# THE LESSON OF THIS CENTURY

Karl Popper has been known for more than half a century as a defender of freedom and an impartial critic of all forms of totalitarianism. He was an indefatigable opponent of the fashionable and the obscurantist in all intellectual fields – religion, nationalism, ideology – and the author of an extensive and influential critique of Marxism (*The Open Society and Its Enemies*).

In *The Lesson of this Century* his purpose is to warn us against the increasing violence and egoism of our society, which imperil democracy. What solutions can we offer to the problems of the environment, demography and corruption? How can we prevent the violence our society engenders? How can we preserve our democratic system while at the same time paving the way for global peace? Popper believes that the philosopher has a duty to intervene in politics and he utters a clear call to all of us to recognize our responsibilities. He reminds us that it is our actions which will create the world of tomorrow.

The interviews in this volume were originally given to the Italian journalist Giancarlo Bosetti, and have been translated here by Patrick Camiller. The volume also includes an interview not previously available in English about the dangers of television and the responsibilities of its makers.

# THE LESSON OF THIS CENTURY

With two talks on freedom and
the democratic state

*Karl Popper*

London and New York

First published 1997

First published in paperback 2000
by Routledge
11 New Fetter Lane, London EC4P 4EE

Simultaneously published in the USA and Canada
by Routledge
29 West 35th Street, New York, NY 10001

*Routledge is an imprint of the Taylor & Francis Group*

© The Estate of Sir Karl Popper 1992
translation © 1997 Patrick Camiller

Typeset by BC Typesetting
Printed and bound in Great Britain by MPG Books

*British Library Cataloguing in Publication Data*
A catalogue record for this book is available from
the British Library

*Library of Congress Cataloguing in Publication Data*
A catalogue record for this book is available from
the Library of Congress

ISBN 0–415–12959–1

# CONTENTS

# CONTENTS

## Two talks

# INTRODUCTION

## *Giancarlo Bosetti*

At one point in this interview, we were about halfway through a long working session in Karl Popper's house at Kenley, a small Surrey town an hour or so from London. As he was again taking me through the core of his critique of Marxism, he stood up from the table and asked me to follow him into the drawing-room-cum-library. We went around a grand piano that was completely covered with books, some still open. The bulkiest of them, however, were placed on metal rests. I looked here and there at the books, curious to know what he was then working on (the pre-Socratic philosophers, the autobiography of the Dalai Lama, the Cuban missile crisis). But Popper took me by the arm and led me to the back of the room, near the shelves devoted to Marx which contained many nineteenth-century English and German editions in gold-embossed leather binding. It was the oldest part of the library, at the opposite end from where the 89-year-old philosopher kept copies of his own works in every language. He showed me the volumes of *Capital* on which he had worked since the age of 17, but that was not the reason why we had left the table. What he pulled out next was a shorter and slimmer volume: the English edition of *The Poverty of Philosophy*, published in 1913. He flicked through the pages, knowing just what he was looking for, then showed it to me on page 117. 'Let's see what it says here.' He read out one of the last sentences in the book that Marx had published in Paris in 1847, as a polemic against Proudhon's *Philosophy of Poverty* of a year earlier. The theme was the 'emancipation of the oppressed class', the proletariat, which 'implies necessarily the creation of a new society'. For this to happen:

1

it is necessary that the productive powers already acquired and the existing social relations should no longer be capable of existing side by side. . . . The organization of revolutionary elements as a class supposes the existence of all the productive forces which could be engendered in the bosom of the old society.

But from this famous passage, which introduced the concept of 'total revolution' and heralded the end of all antagonism, Popper wanted to emphasize one precise point – as if he saw in it a rending flash, as if the key question capable of bringing down the whole theoretical edifice had appeared for a moment in Marx's head. And he read these three lines: 'Does this mean that after the fall of the old society there will be a new class domination culminating in a new class power?'

The question probably contains the nucleus of the problem of communism, in that the very idea of ending all social and political conflict proved incompatible with democracy, with the principle of freedom of opposition and everything that follows from it. But after the question mark Marx simply replied: 'No.' 'You see,' Popper said, 'he barely touches this vast problem with just one question. And then what does he do? He says "no" – without offering any explanation, without even trying (as he should have done) to show why, to show the basis for such a confident prediction. We know now that Marx's answer proved to be wrong.'

Popper was a great opponent of Marx and communism, of any claim to base a political project on knowledge of the laws of history. As the theorist of the open society, he saw in the events of 1989 and 1991 a confirmation of his main criticisms of Marxism. He first began to formulate them in 1919, at the age of 17, after a brief period in which communist ideology – riding high on the peace programme of the Bolshevik revolutionaries – had enticed him into the 'mousetrap'. He talks about that phase of his life in this interview, which rounds off with new material the account given in his autobiography.[1] His criticisms were already fully expressed in *The Open Society and Its Enemies*, first published in 1945.[2] But the interest of Popper's political ideas today lies not only in reviewing the main points of his attack on Marxism. The reasons for my being there with him were essentially twofold: one related to history, the other to political theory.

The first has to do with the question that, since 1989, I had thought of addressing to a philosopher who, shortly after the October Revolution, criticized Marxist communism in terms now broadly shared across virtually the whole spectrum of political thought. The Communist regime, born at the time of Popper's youth, lasted throughout his long life, almost into his 90s; and very early on he had reached clear conclusions about the nature of the error embodied within it. What I wanted to ask Popper was how he had viewed over the years all those people, especially intellectuals, who had remained firm in the opposite convictions. After all, it had been a very long experience, based upon a theory (Marxist historicism) whose strength and error he had found the means to explain.[3] And I wondered whether its very durability had not induced in him a kind of fatalism or frustration. In the end, what is the use of understanding an error, if it goes on being repeated?

Popper did not want to deal with the question directly, except by making one point that again went over the arguments against historicism. Someone might, in fact, think of him as a man who waited on the river bank for the corpses of his enemies to float by. But no part of this image applies to Popper: neither the corpses nor the enemies, and especially not the river. Not the corpses, because he regarded non-violence as a cornerstone of civilization. Not the enemies, because the friend–enemy polarization of history and politics is precisely one of the main things he holds against Marxism. And not the river, because Popper considers the idea of history as a watercourse with a known source and mouth to be responsible for a huge number of crimes.

> You can study history as much as you want, but the river or anything like that will always be just a metaphor. It has no reality in it. You study what has been in the past, but now that is over and you cannot anticipate anything in order to help it along or for you yourself to swim along with it.

Corresponding to the idea of the open society is Popper's idea of the open future. Much can be learnt from the past, but nothing authorizes us to project it into the future as a way of anticipating events. The claim to know the future course of history empties the present of moral responsibility, transforming people into agents of a 'destiny' that will happen come what may. For Popper's radical anti-historicism, the very notion of a 'meaning' to history, of a 'direction' to human affairs, is a 'dangerous stupidity' because it leads to a legitimation of violence and arbitrariness – the worst that can ever befall us. We can see, then, why Popper refuses to place himself in the position of saying: I knew it would end like that. It is not a question of a display of modesty or of puzzlement at the course of events: Popper is genuinely satisfied with the collapse of communism. The point for him, rather, is that the assurance of riding the wave of history should be combated wherever it manifests itself, not only in politics but in every human domain, even art. Marxism was the bearer of a faith in communism as the real move-ment abolishing the present state of things, on the basis of knowl-edge of historical 'laws' and a teleology that authorized the moulding of social matter. But the fact that it was wrong does not mean that its mirror-image is right; the end of communism is not the fulfilment of other, 'true' laws of history.

In support of this position, which we might describe as anti-necessitarian as well as anti-historicist, Popper makes two state-ments in the interview that deserve close consideration. First, the Soviet regime might have lasted longer still, perhaps forever; it was not some law or destiny but a series of definite events – and definite decisions taken by real-life people at their own risk – which brought about its collapse. Second, Marxist ideology and the existence of a Communist regime implied the necessity of anti-Marxist and anti-communist ideology, so that over the decades of this century a con-frontation developed between two ideologies that 'were both in a sense completely mad'. This last assertion suggests some possible lines of exploration. For if it is agreed that there were elements of 'madness' in both ideologies – without disputing the responsibility that Popper attributes to Marxism – then the final bankruptcy of the regimes inspired by the Marxist project does not imply that the world should he handed over to the opposing ideology, at least not as it was while the conflict was under way. Even if we disregard the reactionary and conservative use made of anti-communism to fight against left-democratic movements which, far from being the same as communism, opposed it in their turn, Popper's statement raises the possibility that liberal thought is assuming, or reassuming, a function which was gradually eroded after the October Revolution.

This brings us to the second reason why I thought that an encoun-ter with Popper's ideas might be of interest today: namely, that we might try to find in his liberalism the outlines of a possible solution to the problem of politics and the Left. For it may be that the long communist parenthesis concealed other possible roads, that major political options capable of fusing principles of freedom with social emancipation were squeezed nearly out of sight by the conflict between anti-communist liberalism and Communism. Perhaps a Left with a democratic, socialist and liberal character – which until now seemed little short of utopian – may now be entering the realm of the possible.

In his autobiography Popper had this to say about the period after he broke with Communism.

> I remained a socialist for several years, even after my rejection of Marxism; and if there could be such a thing as socialism combined with individual liberty, I would be a socialist still. For nothing could be better than living a modest, simple, and free life in an egalitarian society. It took some time before I recognized this as no more than a beautiful dream; that freedom is more important than equality; that the attempt to realize equality endangers freedom; and that, if freedom is lost, there will not even be equality among the unfree.[4]

Probably Popper would still endorse those words he wrote in 1974: the combination of socialism with individual liberty is no more than a dream. But it would appear from the interview that he does not dismiss out of hand the possibility and necessity of political action – if, that is, instead of asking about the balance between liberty and equality, we focus our questions on the balance between the market and social intervention. His perspective then seems quite remote from hands-off liberalism. It is revealing that he criticizes Gorbachev for trying to establish a stock market in Moscow before the political reforms needed to get the rule of law off the ground. And it is also indicative of strongly interventionist leanings that he provocatively calls for censorship of the mass media to help educate people in non-violence. In The Open Society Popper's thinking on this matter – the balance between state and market – already seemed favourable in many respects to an interventionist, democratic and gradualist conception of political action, but it would not be easy to find there any suggestions for a political agenda as strong as the ones he expressed in this interview. In fact, these new suggestions presuppose an ends-oriented function of government, nationally and internationally (elimination of atomic weapons, population control, education), which is hard to reconcile, not with the 'open society', but with a liberalism bent on limiting the field of public action. These differences are to be explained not only by the nature

5

of the problems facing us today, but also by the end of a system of communist states.

That the end of Communism has major consequences both in public life and at the level of ideas, especially in the vast area of liberal theory, was made even clearer in recent statements by Isaiah Berlin, a figure similar to Popper in many ways politically. Berlin, being seven years younger than Popper, did not go through a brief period of allegiance to Marxism and Communism. When he was a child, his family enthusiastically supported the democratic February Revolution in Russia, but were directly hit by the coming to power of the Bolsheviks. Berlin's attitude to Marxism, and the evolution of his own political thought, have now been amply reconstructed in an interview with Steven Lukes.[5] The famous essay on 'Two Concepts of Liberty',[6] in which the historian of ideas first drew the distinction between positive liberty and negative liberty, was mainly intended to warn against the dangers of a political project centred on the positive liberty to do and to be – that is, against the dangers of asserting which qualities and contents should be attributed to human existence. Berlin's main target was precisely the Marxist project, and in opposition to it he defended the bulwark of negative liberty (that lack of restrictions which, ultimately coincides with laissez-faire economics). For the Berlin of the *Four Essays*, then, the balance was decidedly on the side of negative liberty; the communist regimes were the main danger to be removed, and it was positive liberty that was responsible for every evil. But today he declares: 'I should have said more clearly that positive liberty is as noble and fundamental an ideal as negative liberty.'[7] For Berlin too, a major exponent of nineteenth-century liberalism, it is as necessary to invest political action with substantive goals and content (which is the characteristic approach of the Left) as it is to defend the principles of individual liberty against the exactions of power.[8]

The historic turn of 1989 in Eastern Europe thus seems to have had important consequences for political thought. The ending of the threat represented by authoritarian political systems and command economies also seems to have ended that repugnance for political intervention in the society and economy which had pervaded most of liberal thought. No longer is the public/private polarity overlaid by the polarity of socialist system and capitalist system. To be sure, the social and political demands made independently by the Western socialist and democratic movement (and by the Left in general) were quite a different matter from the planned economies in the East and the policies of the ruling Communist Parties. And yet, as many calls to extend the sphere of public action were fatally lured into the orbit of communism, they came to be dismissed as authoritarian, even if this meant forgoing various political decisions that needed to be taken. It is easy enough to see how the shadow of 'actually existing socialism', with the threat of incipient totalitarianism and a stifling of private initiative and individual freedoms, was cast over policies of full employment, labour protection or social insurance. And the fact that particular private interests deliberately cultivated this association – when the 'communist' threat at most involved extending the welfare-state and redistributive measures – did little to mitigate its effects. For the presence of the communist regimes in the magnetic field fundamentally disturbed – in comparison with an ideal situation – the swinging of the pendulum between public and private, political action and inaction, state and market, Left and Right. It needs to be explored, of course, whether there was also an influence in the opposite direction (direct impact of the Eastern regimes on the politics of Western countries, and, above all, the role of communist ideology in animating part of the West European labour movement – including, for example, the attraction of the Stalin myth in the years following the Second World War). But the point to be stressed here is that liberal thought, in the broadest sense of the term, seems to be shifting more easily in the current situation towards interventionism – as if it were finally possible to move into a space which, though seen as beneficial, was previously deemed too dangerous to occupy.

The political priorities for today that Popper lists in this interview assume a really major legitimation of public action, especially as regards education in non-violence; we have already seen that he goes so far as to call for children to be protected by censorship. Even if his political conclusion is not accepted,[9] the move is important which allows him to make this demand without deviating in any way from his 'liberal nature'. This is made possible by a concept of the law-based state not only as an authority ensuring that the individual is protected from violence, but also as the result of a civilizing process based upon a general aversion to violence and general agreement to avoid it. And this raises the question of the culture, formative development and ethical norms in the light of which citizens generally behave, relate to one another, and bring up their children. For Popper, the rule of law is an absolute priority: if the percentage of people breaking the general agreement rises above a certain limit, the law-based state itself becomes at risk and may even collapse. The more widespread violence is in society, and the weaker the general agreement to eliminate it, the more it will be necessary to adopt political measures of a repressive type. The elimination of violence – which Popper regards as the hallmark of the law-based state – may be furthered by such measures, but the path of defending and cultivating people's natural propensity to non-violence appears more consistent with a liberal point of view. Popper thinks that firm control of the media, including censorship, is indispensable to halt a process of degeneration – and that it should go together with educational policies in support of the rule of law.

The concept of the rule of law therefore comes to include the 'social substance', in the sense of a cross-generational stratification of culture and ethics. And the protection of the rule of law legitimizes political action to reconstitute and renew the social substance that keeps it alive. It has to be asked whether, by the same token, the concept of the rule of law cannot be extended to all the basic elements of the civilizing process: not only the attitude of citizens to non-violence in social relations, but also the minimum provision with income, culture, information and civic spirit, which form the conditions for participation in public life. Support for the rule of law, defence and development of its social underpinnings, furtherance of the civilizing process – these may perhaps indicate a way of defining all the goals of political action. It is not out of the question that the Left's own thinking, its own search for syntheses to define its role on a new basis, may find something useful, at least methodologically, in the arguments that Popper develops in these pages on the rule of law. With the collapse of the socialist utopia, and the failure of a historical experiment for which it was the goal, it seems inevitable that the Left must give up the idea of redemption in an alternative society. In the past, the Left has proved capable of equipping public action with fresh moral resources, with a commitment to concrete improvements in society, and with the driving force for men and women to pursue broader aims than the ones simply identifiable with their immediate interests. Reflection on the ideas which Popper presents here and elsewhere,[10] may help us to define our goals more adequately. And his conception of the rule of law may usefully be compared with the idea of the Left as a force promoting rights, a bearer of the striving towards the achievement and development of citizenship.[11]

To assist the reader's understanding of Popper's ideas on democracy, the media and the distinction between the minimal and paternalist state, two previously unpublished talks have been included: 'Considerations on the Theory and Practice of the Democratic State' (1988) and 'Freedom and Intellectual Responsibility' (1989). In the first of these, more extensively than in the interview, Popper criticizes the conception of democracy as 'people's rule' and takes up again his famous distinction between the question of *who* rules and the question of *how* government is effected. Given the emphasis we have already noted in liberal thought, there is special importance in the pages where Popper, with Kant's help, tries to find a balance between a negative conception of the protection of liberty, and the necessity of legitimizing government intervention on a relatively large scale. On the one side are the well-founded claims of the idea of a minimal state, against any aberrant use of the public power to dictate the rules of happiness for the citizens; on the other are the ravages of a maximal or paternalist state that stamps out freedom. But in the cramped space between the two conceptions, Popper insists on the obvious fact that public action cannot, on moral grounds, dispense with placing limitations on the freedom of citizens. The difficulty lies in the fact that 'unfortunately ... in principle as well as for moral reasons, things do not work without paternalism'. Whether it is a question of making seat-belts compulsory, banning smoking in public places, making provisions for national defence or public order, or raising taxation to pay for the welfare state, political action inevitably distances itself from an abstractly conceived minimal state. Our main concern, then, should be to control the extent of this paternalism – for example, by setting the criterion: 'No more paternalism than that which is morally necessary.' It is necessary to maintain the utopian ideal of the minimal state, 'if only as a regulative principle', so as to reach a compromise where 'instead of a superiority in principle of the ministate over the moral claims of the paternalist state, we find ourselves back with the old opposition between state and freedom and with Kant's anti-dictatorial rule of not limiting freedom any more than we must'.

The part of our interview in which Popper discusses the Soviet decline and the role of Andrei Sakharov (before the turn that led to his becoming a supporter of radical democratic change in the USSR)[12] has given rise to considerable polemic.[13] His charges against the Russian scientist are very serious and unexpected, representing a dramatic reversal of the judgement he made in a speech in New York in 1981 in honour of Sakharov's sixtieth birthday. His account of the Cuban missile crisis, of Khrushchev's intentions, and of the way in which Sakharov supposedly went beyond the call of his duties as a nuclear physicist, is in conflict with the verdict of historians and scientists. But it may help to recall that Popper, in his New York speech, hailed Sakharov as a 'great thinker, a great humanitarian, a great hero, and, above all, truthful and truth-seeking'. At that time, of course, the Russian scientist's key role in the development of the hydrogen bomb was already well known, but Popper thought that his behaviour had been the same as that of the Western *Bulletin of Atomic Scientists* group, whose involvement in the development of nuclear weapons went together with an awareness of the problems they posed to humanity. At least 'since 1957,' Popper argued, 'Sakharov has dedicated his life to doing everything possible to reduce the most terrible danger to mankind'; and he still agreed with the reasons for which Sakharov had been awarded the Nobel Peace Prize in 1975. In his eyes, moreover, Sakharov was the very model of a man who is tolerant and admits his mistakes; his capacity 'to change his mind radically' marked the decisive difference 'between a dogmatic mind and a critical mind'.[14] This constantly critical attitude to one's own theory, which is unfortunately very rare, was said to be displayed by Sakharov not only in the scientific field, but also in social and political theory. At that moment, Popper was evidently ignorant of what he might have learnt from Sakharov's *Memoirs*,[15] beginning with a clearer idea of his position (mirrored by the American 'hawk' Teller rather than Oppenheimer) in the Soviet debate that had led to the decision to produce the 'big bomb'.[16]

Finally, we cannot fail to mention the silence with which Italian culture, both left and right, confronted Popper's thought, at least until the translation of *The Open Society and Its Enemies* in 1974.[17] One reason for this was the hegemony of the historicism, both Marxist and non-Marxist, which the Viennese philosopher took so severely to task. And another was the length of time that left-wing culture in Italy and elsewhere took to free itself from the burden of Stalinism.

# INTERVIEW I (1991)

# 1

# PACIFISM, WAR, THE ENCOUNTER WITH COMMUNISM

*I think we should begin this interview with the essential point: your critique of Marxism which you expressed most thoroughly in your most important book,* The Open Society and Its Enemies. *Would you explain how and when you conceived the core of this critique, how and when you became convinced of the necessity of that attack on the 'false prophets', from Plato to Marx by way of Hegel, which you developed systematically in the book you published in 1945.*

Actually, this question takes me very far back, to July 1919, when I was not yet 17 years old. Of course, I did not so very quickly reach the position that I argued in *The Open Society*; but it was before my seventeenth birthday, in July 1919, that I decided to review my attitude to Marxism with a view to criticizing it. And not long afterwards, in February 1920, I achieved essentially the position which I have, of course, been further developing all my life. So you see, it was very long ago. And I should say there are very few people today who can remember these things. It was the time shortly after the First World War.

*What attitude did you have to the war?*

I had been a pacifist as a child, before the First World War. My parents were pacifists: my father had pacifist literature in his library and he was strongly opposed to Austrian militarism. When the war broke out, I was frightened and alarmed by the fact that most people around me – friends of my family, and so on – did a 180-degree turn and became supporters of the war. We were on holiday at the end of July 1914, and my father sent me a letter from Vienna in which he said he couldn't come to visit us because unfortunately – that was the word he used, 'unfortunately' – it was going to be

13

war. The letter was written on the day before my birthday and – from what I can remember – the war actually began on my birthday. So he saw some hours before that the war was about to start. Soon afterwards I went back to Vienna, where everyone at school was supporting war.

*Were you too influenced by that climate?*

I wasn't completely immune from it. I was influenced a little, but only to the extent of hoping for a quick peace in which, of course, the Central Powers would have won. At the same time, I did not think of anything like a real victory, as most other people did.

*Do you really have a clear memory of what you thought about the war at that time?*

I know all these things because I wrote a poem, of which I still remember a few lines. It was called 'The Celebration of the Peace', and in it I said that the enemies had all gone home and we now had peace. Nothing in this poem said that the peace was a triumph, or anything like that. But I also know that it was written in October 1914 or thereabouts, and that already early in the New Year I was ashamed of having anticipated victory enough to say that our enemies went home defeated – which was the idea originally contained in the poem. So very soon I became, let us say, a real opponent of the idea of defeating the enemies of the Central Powers.

*What led you to become more sharply opposed to the war?*

In 1915 or '16 I had long conversations with my father about what was likely to happen. The real point was that, being a child, I was sure that those in the right would win – which is, of course, very naive. Anyway, early in 1915, after the invasion of Belgium, I found out that Germany had violated certain treaties, and this convinced me not only that our side was in the wrong but that we must therefore lose the war.

*Going forward a little, can you remember when it was that you first heard about the ideas of the October Revolution?*

It was at the time of the talks at Brest-Litovsk between Russia and the Central Powers that led to the famous treaty. I was a little more than 15 and was very impressed by the speeches made by the Russians there. Trotsky, of course, was the main speaker, and strangely enough outlines of various speeches were printed in Austria (probably in Germany too, though I'm not sure). This was what first attracted me towards the Communists. I also had a Russian-born friend who had been a student leader during the 1905 Revolution, and he warned me that the Communists were people who would do anything whatsoever if it suited their party. But the truth is that I took his warning with a little scepticism, because of the speeches at Brest-Litovsk.

*So what attracted you about Communism was that the Russian speeches talked of peace and scorned the idea of military victory?*

I was already faced, as it were, with the main problem that has always interested me since then: Communism, yes or no?

*And you became a Communist.*

Shortly after the peace, in 1919, I went to the Communist Party office and offered them my services as an errand boy. Among the leaders there were three children of an Austrian philosopher Rudolf Eisler: Gerhardt, Hans and Fritti (short for Elfride) Eisler, whose married name was Friedlander, although she may already have been divorced by then. Gerhardt later became the main leader of the American Communists and was expelled from the United States after the Second World War. His younger brother, Hans, became one of the most important musicians in East Germany. And Fritti Friedlander, under the name Ruth Fischer, became one of the leaders of German Communism.

*I don't remember your mentioning these figures in your auto-biography, where you speak in general of your 'Communist friends'. Why did you want to name them this time?*

It was an interesting meeting I had with them. They were very nice to me, spoilt me a little, and at first I trusted them. But very soon I found that a telegram from Moscow was enough for them to turn 180 degrees and say the opposite of what they had been saying the day before. Their attitude to people could also change completely from one day to the next. In other words, they had only one principle, and that was to support Moscow absolutely through thick and thin, without the slightest wavering. So when I found that out, my attitude to Communism was thrown into crises.

*As I understand it, the Eisler brothers were people with a certain intellectual standing. So their conduct must have driven you to seek the*

15

*reasons for such sudden turns not in any character defects of theirs but in the depths of communist ideology. Was this how you began the search that you completed in* The Open Society? *Perhaps this is the point at which you should explain your central criticism of Marxism.*

Yes, you are right. Marx had predicted that socialism or communism – I won't make a distinction now – must come as a form of the dictatorship of the proletariat. It was a necessity of history which could be established with certainty through the study of history and economics. It could be proved. Communism was something that *must* come. Capitalism was an evil form of society: it *had to* end, it *had to* be overthrown by the Communists. That was bound to happen. After that there would be a wonderful society, a completely new society in which all people would love one another and peace would reign on earth. That was the main thing. And that is why I call this doctrine a trap, a kind of mousetrap. And I was the mouse.

*In your autobiography you describe how you eventually 'grasped the heart of the Marxist argument'. 'It consists', you wrote, 'of a historical prophecy, combined with an implicit appeal to the following moral law:* Help to bring about the inevitable!'[1] *Can you say a little more about this idea of a 'trap'?*

Communist doctrine, which promises the coming of a better world, claims to be based on knowledge of the laws of history. So it was obviously the duty of everybody, especially of somebody like me who hated war and violence, to support the party which would bring about, or help to bring about, the state of affairs that must come in any case. If you knew this yet resisted it, you were a criminal. For you resisted something that had to come, and by your resistance you made yourself responsible or co-responsible for all the terrible violence and all the deaths which would happen when communism inevitably established itself. It *had to* come; it *had to* establish itself. And we had to hope there would be the minimum resistance, with as few people sacrificed as possible.

So everyone who had understood that the inevitability of socialism could be scientifically proved had a duty to do everything to help it come about. This was why the leaders of Communism did those strange things and contradicted themselves from one day to the next. All this was justified, because they were helping to establish communist power; that was the crucial question of history, the main reason for every action, the justification for every choice.

It was clear that people, even leaders, must make mistakes – but that was a small matter. The main point was that the Communists were fighting for what *had to* come in the end. That was what I meant by speaking of a trap, and I was myself for a time caught in the trap.

*For a few months. But then you changed your mind. What else had happened – apart from the sudden shifts of your friends?*

Various things began to happen which I found very questionable. In Vienna, where several Communists were being held in the main police building, the Party decided to call a demonstration for their release which was mainly attended by young people. The police opened fire and six young demonstrators were killed. I saw it happen: I was there. And then I began to think. The Party leaders took the attitude that the more terrible the things that happened, the better it was; it would all help to excite the fury which is necessary for the revolution, for the great revolution. So they didn't regret what happened, but I did feel a responsibility for those young people.

*This point is not at all clear, either in your autobiography, or in earlier interviews where you talked about that time in your life. For in essence you decided to distance yourself from the Communists while some young Communists were being killed by the police in Vienna; in that case, the Communists were the victims, not the ones doing the shooting. And it was precisely then that you gave up Communism. Isn't that strange?*

I felt a kind of responsibility. I felt it was all right to sacrifice oneself, to place oneself in danger; but we were encouraging others to place themselves in danger and to be shot at, and we had no right to do that. The Party leaders had no right to tell other people that they should sacrifice themselves or risk their lives. Those young demonstrators were workers, and we were intellectuals who believed we could judge and, so to speak, underwrite Marxism. By then I was already at the university. We were students, we could read thick books, and we thought we had the right to tell people: this is how things are; Communism must come, and we must bring it about in a fight. So I realized that we were responsible and I began to ask myself whether things really were as we said they were. Did I really know that the Marxists proofs that Communism must come were valid? Was I able to guarantee that? Could I really go to people who could not themselves read Marx and say: I have critically tested and checked Marx, and I can assure you that what he says is true, that his proofs are valid, that communism must come and we will be victorious, so all these consequences follow?

*And what did you do then?*

I decided to study Marx really thoroughly, as I hadn't done before. I had used him, I had had to use him, but it was a very superficial knowledge that I had. So now I thought I really must examine whether his theory could be proved.

# 2

# THE MAIN CRITICISMS OF MARXISM

*That was when you began to work out the core of your critique of Marxism. How did you go about it?*

I began to study *Capital* and realized that its main arguments were the following. Number one: capitalism cannot be reformed, but can only be destroyed; if one wishes to have a better society it must be destroyed. Number two: the argument of increasing misery, the idea that the workers' lot will grow worse and worse; and that is why it is necessary to destroy capitalism. A third very interesting and very important argument is that capitalists cannot be individually blamed; they are themselves victims of the system. It is important to recall this, because I found that of course the Communists never mentioned it. They also blamed the capitalists personally and tried to arouse personal hatred of them, whereas Marx had said that capitalism was a kind of machine in which the capitalists were caught as much as the workers, unable to do anything but what the machine made them do. Marx actually called 'vulgar Marxism' the view that capitalists were bad people who maliciously exploited others. I found here an interesting argument against the main propaganda of the Communists, which precisely was characterized by 'vulgar Marxism'. And of course, the Party thought it had the right to uphold it, because the Party had a right to do anything that helped it pursue the goal of revolution. Here was the trap again. The Party's function was such that it had the right to arouse as much hatred as it could in order to hasten the coming of communism. That was the basic analysis I reached at that time through my study of Marx.

*But the main elements of your critique of Marxism are not all there. Others came later.*

There is one other important argument, in particular, which I found only after the publication of *The Open Society*. It is that capitalism, as Marx describes it, has never existed. It is just an invention, a dream a devil dreamt up. Of course, there were always rich people and poor people, and the poor people always suffered, and there was always a moral demand to help the poor, to help the underdog. And still today I feel we should help the underdog. But I don't think it is the workers who are the underdogs today – we'll see later who I think *are*. There are still poor people today, of course, but the problem of hunger and of the workers' condition is no longer as it was in Marx's day. I don't deny that society was then in many respects very bad, but it was not what Marx described as capitalism; it could be reformed, whereas his main thesis was that it could only be destroyed. Later, he himself admitted that perhaps in England – and only in England – the social revolution would come without violence; he didn't put it that society could be reformed, but that was what it amounted to saying.

The fact is that during Marx's lifetime tremendous reforms, great and very important reforms, did take place, both in England and especially in Germany under Bismarck. So what he said about capitalism was actually refuted by the facts in his own lifetime. So the thing he called capitalism, a society in which both workers and capitalists were caught in a machinery that must make things worse and worse, never existed. *Ein Kapitalist schlägt vielen tot* – one capitalist slays many others – was one of the many formulations expressing his idea that fewer and fewer capitalists would be left, and almost everybody would then be a victim and a worker. But that kind of society never existed, and we make a mistake if we call ours a capitalistic society in the Marxian sense, because the Marxian term is and always has been inapplicable to it. This is my main criticism of Marxism, but there is also another.

Marx had the idea that the capitalists are the hidden dictators of the state, that under capitalism the state is a dictatorship and that capitalists are the dictators. This is an absolute dream. Never has a society existed in which the capitalists had the politically decisive power; things have always been much more complicated. It has to be said that Marx brought into the social sciences and historical science the very important idea that economic conditions are of great importance in the life of society – as opposed to what historians, for example, had previously believed. There was nothing like serious economic history before Marx – that is true. But like others who have made a discovery, he exaggerated it enormously and explained everything in terms of economics. He believed that the economy was all-important, and this is certainly a mistake. For society is a highly complex reality: there are other things in it such as religion, nationality, friendship or the old school tie. In Vienna, for example, nearly all the Social Democratic leaders came from the same class in school and remained friends afterwards. And in England, Oxford University had a tremendous influence on politics: nearly all the politicians of all parties were former friends from the university. All these factors play a role, and the simple idea of a dictatorship of the capitalists has never corresponded at all to the real state of things.

# 3

# THE YEAR 1962
## Sakharov, Khrushchev and the Soviet decline

*We have clarified your critique of the 'mousetrap', and you have told us how you were caught in it and broke free. Let us now turn to the question of Soviet Communism, and how whole countries and millions of people have come out of it.*

I think the reasons for the Soviet decline are very interesting, but we should start by considering what happened to Marxism in Russia. There were important developments in both Russia and Italy, but it was above all in Germany, through such figures as Karl Kautsky and Eduard Bernstein, that Marxism was first seriously studied and made into a kind of philosophy or many-sided intellectual doctrine, with an extensive literature. In Russia, of course, with the Communists in power, it became a system in which students at every level of education were indoctrinated. But when we come to the time of, say, Khrushchev, nobody in the Communist leadership took this seriously except as a means of keeping things going. Only one thing was taken seriously: that capitalism must be destroyed. The enemy was capitalism, and capitalism became more or less identified with America and England. These were the great capitalist countries, which had to be destroyed. All the rest of the theory disappeared, but not this. In Khrushchev's memoirs there is a very simple formulation which is the key to the whole book: 'The liquidation of the capitalist system is the crucial question in the development of society.'[1] Or he might have said: 'in the development of history' – the meaning would be the same.

*Doubts have been raised about the authenticity of that book.*

There is no doubt in my mind that it is genuine. It would be an incredible achievement if someone were to have forged it. It is an immensely detailed book of more than 600 pages, including such things as telephone conversations with Stalin, and to fake it would have required years and years of research. Besides, this has never really been seriously suggested, although the history of the book is strange. It was smuggled out of the Soviet Union and, to my knowledge, first published in English. I think all people who know something about Russia consider it to be genuine; we can assume that it really is the story of his life and opinions. It does a lot to help us understand the history of the twentieth century, and especially the great turning point represented by the Cuban crisis of 1962.

*Why do you think that was so important?*

In my view, the Soviet Union lost the Cold War at that point, when there was an attempt to destroy America. That was when the only remaining idea of the Marxist regime failed; it was the beginning of the decline that led to the general collapse.

*And why did it happen just then?*

It was the first time the Soviet Union had ever had the possibility of destroying the United States. The Soviets had had no hope of achieving their aims, the aims set them by history, until they had the Sakharov bomb of which the Russian physicist speaks in his memoirs. It was this book which changed my mind on Sakharov as a person. I think he was at that time criminally irresponsible.

*You are speaking of a man who was awarded the Nobel Peace Prize in 1975, a man you yourself praised to the skies in New York in 1981 as 'a great thinker, a great humanitarian, a great hero'.[2] Everyone knew then that Sakharov had created the H-bomb. So why have you now changed your mind?*

I still have a very high opinion of what he did in later years, but his own book contains things which forced me to change my mind about the earlier period. The problem of Sakharov is very interesting. We cannot go into every aspect here: that will be a matter for historians. But I would just like to quote this, for example: 'I had decided', he writes, 'to test a "clean" version [of the bomb]: this would reduce its force, but the Big Bomb would still greatly surpass any previously tested charge and would be several thousand times more powerful than the bomb dropped on Hiroshima.'[3] 'Several thousand times more powerful.' What does 'several' mean? I assume it means at least three. That is a conservative assumption if one

considers the following facts. Sakharov has, I think, many questionable points in his character, but he writes the truth: he does not lie
and he does not exaggerate. So if he says 'several thousand times' –
about a version of the bomb slightly weaker than he could in fact
produce – then it was at least 3,000 times more powerful than the
Hiroshima bomb. Sakharov had worked long under Stalin, coopera-
ted with Beria, and repeatedly had hour-long private conversations
with Beria in connection with building the bomb. Anyway, after
years of tests, the really decisive one took place in 1961 – in September, I think. Khrushchev knew all about this, of course, and he
recalls: 'It was during my visit to Bulgaria that I had the idea of
installing missiles with nuclear warheads in Cuba without letting
the United States find out that they were there until it was too late
to do anything about them.'[4]

*The bomb had passed the test and Khrushchev had the Cuba idea. As
historians have shown, the idea came to him in Bulgaria when he
was thinking about the American warheads sited a short distance
away, in Turkey. So what was new?*

One thing that was new was the size of the Soviet nuclear potential.
A year after the bomb was tested, Khrushchev went ahead with his
idea. The bombs were taken to Cuba and thirty-eight were already
there, though not yet ready to be fired, when the United States
found out. Khrushchev writes about this: 'We hadn't had time to
deliver all our shipments to Cuba.' But he adds: 'We had installed
enough missiles already to destroy New York, Chicago, and the
other huge industrial cities, not to mention a little village like
Washington.'[5] And although he would later speak differently, he
goes on here: 'I don't think America had ever faced such a real
threat of destruction as at that moment.'[6] Let us do a quick calcula-
tion. If each of the thirty-eight warheads already in Cuba had 3,000
times more power than the bomb used at Hiroshima, then the
destructive potential was 114,000 times bigger than what is needed
to destroy a city.

*It was already known that the history of the world was close to cata-
strophe at that moment ...*

But what President Kennedy didn't know was the real size of the
Soviet nuclear potential. Nor was this known to his brother, Robert
Kennedy, who played a major role in the crisis and wrote an impor-
tant book about it.[7] They knew it was big, of course, but I don't

think they had any idea of the real size. That comes only from the information Sakharov gives us in the passage I quoted. I haven't seen it anywhere else, not even in Michael Beschloss's very well-documented work, which is the most recent on the topic.[8]

*Do you mean that no historian has yet noticed those words of Sakharov's?*

I don't want to attack the historians; they haven't had very much time. But I haven't read any review of the Sakharov book which mentions that passage.

*Did you change your mind about Sakharov because of the size of his bomb? After all, no one ever doubted that it was immensely destructive.*

Let me draw your attention to another passage from his book. 'After the test of the Big Bomb, I was concerned that the military couldn't use it without an effective carrier (a bomber would be too easy to shoot down).'[9] So, Sakharov was 'concerned' that the bomb could not be used, even though that wasn't his task. But let us see what else he says:

> I dreamed up the idea of a giant torpedo, launched from a submarine and fitted with an atomic-powered jet engine that would convert water to steam. The targets would be enemy ports several hundred miles away. Naval experts assured us that the war at sea would be won if we could destroy the enemy's harbours. The torpedoes' bodies would be made sturdy enough to withstand exploding mines and to pierce anti-torpedo nets. When they reached their targets, the 100-megaton charges would explode both underwater and in the air, causing heavy casualties.[10]

You can see here that Sakharov was not just a passive worker doing anything he was ordered to do, but that he took on an active role. He adds:

> I consulted with Rear Admiral Fomin at an early stage of the torpedo project. He was shocked and disgusted by the idea of merciless mass slaughter, and remarked that the officers and sailors of the fleet were accustomed to fighting only armed adversaries, in open battle. I was utterly abashed, and never discussed the project with anyone else. I'm no longer worried

that someone may pick up on the idea; it doesn't fit in with current military doctrines, and it would be foolish to spend the extravagant sums required.[11]

'Utterly abashed'! That is the only place in the whole book where Sakharov says anything like that. After having dreamt up this frightful thing which could destroy New York in one blow, he listens, he consults, he goes to the fleet, he consults an admiral, and the admiral says: No, that isn't the way we fight. And Sakharov is utterly abashed!

*You knew Einstein personally. Do you think his attitude to building and using the bomb was essentially any different?*

It was very different. Einstein signed his letter in support of developing the bomb because he thought the Germans were building one of their own. So he signed the letter to defend America. But Sakharov, at the time we are talking about, was still a Communist who wanted to 'liquidate' capitalism, to use Khrushchev's words. He was not just a passive tool of aggressive leaders. He was, on the contrary, fully convinced of the idea that capitalism must be liquidated. He was 39 years old when the bomb was tested, and 40 when he went to see this admiral.

*You are accusing Sakharov of terrible things. Why have you changed the judgement you made ten years ago? What is the point of putting the early Sakharov on trial again?*

What all this shows is that a man of great intelligence like Sakharov, a man who was obviously capable of seeing that the Soviet regime had made Russia a terrible place – and did see it a few years later – could nevertheless be so blind. In his book he says: 'I was just a worker' – which is what all the German war criminals argued. And when he once said to Khrushchev: 'I shall do my duty', this was not because he doubted whether he should produce the bomb, but because of a dispute over testing. Sakharov realized that every test of his superbomb would mean thousands of people getting cancer from the radiation, and so he tried to persuade Khrushchev not to carry out the tests. But Khrushchev angrily told him not to get mixed up in what was a 'political' not a 'scientific' issue. And that was when Sakharov said: 'I shall do my duty.' There are many more things to be said about Sakharov; his *Memoirs* will need to be closely looked at.

*But there is also another side to Sakharov. He changed his views, showed great courage, challenged the regime, and became a supporter of the democratic turn.*

It is clear from page 221 of his *Memoirs* that the designing of a new kind of weapon to destroy America, the torpedo, was his own initiative which he had not been asked to come up with. He too was caught in the 'mousetrap', obsessed with this idea of liquidating capitalism. It was like a kind of intellectual black hole, based on the principle that someone knows the laws determining the necessary and inevitable course of future history. And you can't say of a 40-year-old that he's too young to judge. It is quite true that he later changed his views. But how shall I put it: if a man kills you when he's 40 and says a few years later that he's sorry and shouldn't have done it, is he any less of a murderer? As I said, I still have a high opinion of Sakharov's later years, but I do have to correct my overall judgement of him. I have to say that he began as a war criminal, and I cannot say that he is, so to speak, fully excused by what he later did.

*But can't you take account of the fact that Sakharov was the child of his times in Russia?*

It is true that his situation made it more difficult to see the 'trap'. I, for example, lived in a free country, a comparatively free country, when I got out of the trap at 17 years of age; but he was in Russia when he got out of it later. You can see here, in the most forceful way imaginable, the power of an ideology over people of extraordinary intelligence, talent and courage. And Sakharov certainly showed that he had the latter.

*Returning to your argument about the Cuban missile crisis, what evidence is there that Khrushchev would have used the bombs first if he had actually managed to deploy them in secret? Was his aim not to hold talks on an equal footing with the Americans (missiles in Cuba against missiles in Turkey)?*

You don't bring something like 114,000 Hiroshima bombs to Cuba in order to reach an agreement with the United States; that's absolute nonsense. If he had had the bombs ready to fire, he would have had to use them, for the Americans would have had to retaliate as quickly as possible. The Soviet leader couldn't have said to Kennedy: 'Look, I have enough here to kill you – what will you give me for it?' Because America could have done nothing else but send their bombs to Cuba as quickly as possible. Is that not clear? There would have been no other choice for America, and Khrushchev must have known that his enemies would have had no choice but to use their nuclear weapons. Anybody who thinks the situation through must be able to see that. I know you have a million in your pocket and I have a gun and you have a gun and I come at you with my gun. I cannot then say: 'I've come to discuss with you whether you should have your gun.' It's just a question of who shoots first.

*You brought up the question of Sakharov and the crisis of 1962 in connection with the decline of the Soviet Union. Could you explain that connection a little more clearly? In your view, the failure of Khrushchev's military venture was the beginning of the end. So do you think that 1962 was the last chance for the Soviet Union to beat the United States?*

The first and the last. The first, because before they had the Sakharov bomb they had no chance to destroy America without a war — which is to say by murder. And the last, because they knew that the Americans would not hesitate if such a situation ever arose again. And with that the sharp decline began.

*So do you think the military balance was the key to the fate of the Soviet Union and Communism?*

Yes, it was. The only basic idea, the last one remaining from the Marxist doctrine, was that capitalism had to be destroyed. And the ruling class of a dictatorship saw itself as the instrument of history through which capitalism would be destroyed and the world saved. But after 1962 they went on producing bombs, all the time knowing that they couldn't use them. That was an absolute intellectual zero point. Their hopes kept deteriorating after that, and now we are in a situation where they have some 1,400 bombs, each equivalent to at least 3,000 Hiroshimas, giving a total of at least 4.2 million Hiroshimas. Each of these bombs may end up on the black market, where the Chinese too could appear as possible competitors. That is the really terrible situation we are facing now.

*We'll come back to this crucial political question. But now I would like to ask you to complete your account of the Soviet decline. You think 1962 was the last chance for a military 'liquidation' of the United States, although many would probably see it instead as the last chance for rough military parity between the USA and the USSR. At any event, the Communist regime lasted a long time after that, and the final turn came only with Gorbachev.*

Only with Gorbachev do we find a man who realizes that he has to change the fundamental assumption of the whole of Russian politics, that they are the people whose mission it is to destroy capitalism – that is, America. Gorbachev has actually been several times to America and seen the reality there; he wants to show his understanding of a free people which is not aggressive towards Russia but hopes that Russia will come to her senses. And Gorbachev made an important statement when he said: 'I want to make the people of the Soviet Union a normal people.' That is one of his few acute formulations: it means that he saw through things and realized that it wasn't a normal people, in which someone like Sakharov could be made aggressive in the highest degree imaginable. You see, Gorbachev's merit was to have understood that his people was not 'normal' whereas the American people was. The attitude is really quite different in America; they do not all the time have this horrible game in their mind. Anyone who knows America will understand what I am saying.

*You recognize that merit in Gorbachev, and yet you don't seem to have a high opinion of him. I have read an interview you gave recently to Riccardo Chiaberge, in which you said that Gorbachev's book* Perestroika *was 'completely empty', 'old hat' and worse, while Yeltsin was 'a man obsessed with his own ego'.*[12]

Yes, I confirm that. I have always said that Gorbachev is probably a man of goodwill but without ideas or plans. You can see from his book that there is really nothing there. But he did understand the difference I just mentioned, and that he needed the help of the United States. As for Yeltsin, the main thing apart from his self-image is his preoccupation with getting revenge against Gorbachev.

*Anyway it is with these people that the reorientation and then dissolution of the Soviet regime have come about. What do you think was the main thing leading to the collapse?*

What brought on the breakdown was the flight of East Germans through Hungary to West Germany. Although the Soviet Union had been reduced to a kind of empty room intellectually, it could have gone on for ever, or at least for a long time. But the decision of the Hungarians to allow GDR citizens and their cars to cross to the West led to the fall of the East German regime, with everything that has followed from it. At that time, there was nothing Gorbachev could have done to avert catastrophe. He would have had to send troops into Hungary, but he was not prepared to do that, and anyway the Americans wouldn't have swallowed it in that situation. So you could say that the key move for the events since 1989 came from Hungary.

# 4

# THE POLITICAL AGENDA TODAY

## The rule of law and children

*We have thus come to the end of the Soviet regime. Could you say what you think are the implications, both for that former model-country itself, and for world politics in general? In terms of political theory, what are the conclusions we should draw?*

The first point is that you cannot make a free-market society from the top down. What you can and should do under all circumstances, what every government has a duty to do, is to try to establish the rule of law. And Russia certainly needs the rule of law, although I have not heard it said anywhere. Let me show you the crass difference between what Gorbachev did and what he should have done. He did something grotesque, ridiculous: he established a stock exchange in Moscow. We have seen pictures of its formal opening, with great celebration under the auspices of the Orthodox Church.

*Why was a Moscow stock exchange grotesque?*

Because there was no stock and no money to buy stock. Neither stocks nor shares, you know; no real money, only roubles. Yet he wanted to have a stock exchange! What Russia needs first are judges who are not politically selected as Party members, judges devoted to the rule of law who know they are responsible for helping the rule of law to exist in the country. So far, judges in the Soviet Union have essentially been instruments of the dictatorship; there has been no code on the basis of which everyone could be assured of a regular trial, and so on. Even Napoleon knew he had to establish a Code if there was to be a free-market society. No one thought you could do without one – not even here in Britain, where there is a long tradition of the rule of law. The need for the rule of law should be obvious, as here too there is a lot of corruption and interfering with

31

the market. The police are constantly having to intervene and look into what happens at the Stock Exchange.

So if even in the West we have to fight for the rule of law, in Russia that should be the first and only task of the government. Instead, they try every way of introducing some new economic system. But that cannot be established from the top, because a free market cannot exist where people have no idea about economics, or do not realize that any kind of business must establish itself by offering something that nobody else offers – new bread, new beans, new apples, and so on. People must be offered something they both need and want, but for that to be possible there must be a mechanism that protects people who buy and sell on the market.

*You are touching on a crucial question for how we think about the world today, one on which there is generally a degree of confusion. It is the question of the relationship between market freedom and state intervention, between defence of free initiative in the economy and the indispensable tasks of public political action. The crisis of the communist planned economies has given a boost to a kind of wild, politically unregulated capitalism which no longer exists – if ever it did – in the Western world. In* The Open Society, *which is where you most directly criticize the social engineering of a totalitarian system, you never embraced a naive view of liberalism as the lack of all state intervention. You even stated your preference for gradualist democratic interventionism, along the lines of Scandinavian social democracy. Let us see whether there are clues here for a view of politics that might be useful for the present and future, both East and West. First of all, what do you think is the right balance between market and social intervention?*

Let me begin by saying that a free market without intervention does not and cannot exist. This makes the whole question different from how it is usually presented.

*Why?*

We have accounts of what used to happen in the Mediterranean markets of Antiquity. Ships came to Athens from Phoenicia and people were buying and selling. But when the Phoenicians took some Greek children back with them, that was the end of it. Of course, the Phoenicians didn't dare return to Athens. Do you see what I am trying to say? The Phoenicians stole, and what they mainly stole were people, and that prevented the stabilization of a market. If a legal system is not first in place, you cannot have a free market. There must be a difference between buying-and-selling and robbing. And this can only be established by a state and by the legal system of a state. Even in a society that has cases of quasi-robbery – that is, of corruption – people scheme and do things that cannot be thought of as pertaining to a free market. The Maxwell affair provides a recent example of this in Britain. In part at least, it too is a business of corruption and stolen money, in the sense that Maxwell got millions from the banks which he was unable to repay. Just imagine an attempt to establish what is called capitalism without a legal system – it would inevitably end in corruption and robbery. So the difference between more and less state intervention is negligible in comparison with the difference between a society with and a society without a legal system.

*You are overturning some ideas which are now quite widespread, especially in the East, about the need to get rid of every function of politics. What consequences does all this have for the evolution of Russian society, in particular?*

I think it will take years to establish a legal system and anything like a free market in the former Soviet Union. First there will be all sorts of adventures. People will come to Russia and go back with a lot of money, no doubt leaving obligations behind them. Only chaos can develop without a legal system: that is my main thesis. But this is all overlooked because people are so influenced by Marxism; they think the economy is everything. They don't think of the legal system, because, according to Marx, legality is robbery in disguise. But that is a very wrong way of looking at it.

*So, in your view, state intervention is decisive for the creation of a legal system and the rule of law, which are essential preconditions of a free market. Let us now see whether the scope of public action can help us in defining the role of the Right and the Left. But do these words, 'Right' and 'Left', still have any meaning for you? Do they mark a permanent division in politics to which it is still useful to refer?*

I do have one great hope. It is that with the disappearance of Marxism, we may succeed in eliminating the pressure of ideologies as the centre of politics. Marxism needed an anti-Marxist ideology, so what you had was the clash between two ideologies which were both in a sense completely mad. There was nothing real behind them – only wrong problems. What I hope from the open society is that we will re-establish a list of priorities of the things which have to be done in society.

*Tell us, then, what is your list of priorities.*

The first point is peace. It means that all the civilized, still civilized societies should perhaps cooperate to buy up the Sakharov bombs, the bombs from China, and so on, that come on to the black market. Perhaps we can buy them. Why shouldn't we buy them? It's probably the best way to get them out. All these countries should co-operate in ensuring, if possible, that the bombs are in the hands of civilized people who can destroy all of them, keeping just a few for security. That would be the first part. And it would not any longer be an ideological point.

The second point would, in my opinion, be to stop the population explosion. It is a truly world issue. All this talk about the environment is nothing if it does not take up the real point behind it. The destruction of the environment comes about only because there are too many people. So this again is a fundamental point on which really everyone should cooperate.

The third main point on which all should cooperate is education. Some years ago, I was asked by the Social Democratic Party in the House of Lords to give them a lecture on the problem. My thesis was that we are educating our children to violence by way of television and other such means. And I said that, very unfortunately, we do need censorship.

*It is surprising that a liberal such as yourself should have said that. The degeneration of the mass media is an objection that is often made in the United States – but also by German cultural criticism – against the permissiveness of liberals. The damage caused by pornography and violence is a particular hobbyhorse of the opponents of liberalism.*

I do not like to say it, precisely because I am a liberal. I am not in favour of censorship. But freedom depends on responsibility. If everyone were responsible and considered the effect on children of what is shown, then we wouldn't need censorship. But unfortunately that is not the case, and meanwhile things have become worse and worse. People want more violence, to see more violence on television. The situation can't go on like this.

I have read in the papers about a boy in Italy who, together with two others, killed his own father because he was stealing his money.[1] More than the case itself, what struck me was the flood of fan letters he received. Now, I ask you, is this not a proof that I was right when I warned that we are educating our children to violence? The fan letters have been coming, of course, from young people who spend hours on end watching television. I have been an educator of children and I know that they do not like violence. When we go to the cinema with children, we can see that they shut their eyes when a dangerous situation arises. But then they are broken in like a horse, and they want to see more and more violence because their feelings of fear and aversion are overcome by habit.

We create with this an impossible situation. The rule of law is there first of all to avoid violence – indeed, that would be a good definition of it. I cannot, according to the law, start punching you around. The freedom of my fists is limited by laws that make hitting you on the nose illegal. That is the fundamental idea of the rule of law. And when we allow the general aversion to violence to be broken down and superseded, we really undermine the rule of law and the general agreement that violence is to be avoided. We undermine our civilization.

*So, the third point in your list of priorities is children's education.*

We have a duty to educate them properly, just as we have to teach them reading and writing and so on. So we have to avoid breaking down the natural resistance that most people have to violence.

*This is a kind of moral interventionism which is quite strange for a liberal such as yourself. Sometimes in recent years – in arguing against environmentalists, for example – you have seemed to favour entrusting the solution of problems to a totally free market. And the degradation of the mass media is an effect of the market.*

The free market is very important, but no more than anything else can it be absolutely free. Absolute freedom is nonsense. Let us take the way Kant formulated this. We need a society in which the freedom of each person is compatible with the freedom of other persons. The compatibility of my freedom with yours depends on our both renouncing violence towards each other. I won't knock you down, and you won't knock me down. We see that our freedom is limited. If we don't see that, then we need there to be laws against violence, against murder. It is always the same. If people do not dream of knocking you down, then there is no need for a law. But if they do dream of knocking you down, there does have to be this kind of interference.

What I say, then, is that if we educate our children better we can have more freedom, but that if we neglect this we have to have less freedom. The rule of law demands non-violence, and if we forget about this then the law will have to interfere more in areas like publication and television. It is a very simple principle which is always the same: to maximize the freedom of each within the limits imposed by the freedom of others. But if we go on as we do now, we shall soon be living in a society where murder is our daily bread.

*You are talking, then, of a political principle which is also a moral principle.*

We have a further moral obligation towards our children, and that is to give them the best we can, including the best influences we can design for their happiness. And, how shall I say, there is really no new principle involved, only the fundamental principle of liberalism that the rule for moving my fist is limited by your nose. So I do not deviate from my liberal principle in demanding that the rule of law should be extended for the protection of our children, who are after all the most important thing we have.

*You have said what are the main priorities you would like to see on the political agenda – peace, stopping the population explosion, and education in non-violence. And you have stressed that they require the cooperation of everyone on all sides. Does this mean that they are neither right nor left?*

Neither right nor left. They could actually supersede the right–left thing to give us what I have called 'social engineering'. That is to say, we have to think what is necessary to achieve these aims. We have to put our aims down, and they really have to be aims for all, not for any particular section of society. Apart from that, we should consider whether there are what I call 'underdogs' – such as cripples or people with mental problems, who are in a very bad situation and certainly should be given special help. All this has to be put into a list of priorities, which should, of course, be open for everyone to debate. In this way we could supersede the horrible party system, which means that the people now in parliament are first of all dependent on their party, and only secondly are there to use their minds for the sake of the population they represent. I think that we should, if possible, go back to a state where MPs say: I am your representative, I belong to no party. That was how things once used to be in this and some other countries. And in my view, the break-down of Marxism is a chance for us to go in that direction. I do hope that some party – it doesn't matter which – will say that for their part they accept this list of priorities. That would make the other parties accept it too, and then we would have a new situation.

*You have now told us your view of democratic interventionism and your list of priorities. On this basis, what kind of political model do you consider most satisfactory for our times: social democracy, liberalism, Western socialism, or some other form of political practice still to be devised?*

A good political model would be a democracy which, in the end, does not see its task as being to establish cultural leadership. It must now be for peace and all the other things I mentioned, but the aim is that people are culturally free and not led by the top. Of course, this means a lot of education, and so on; we have to realize that a great deal of cultural hopes have been destroyed by television. In my youth all manner of things were terribly bad, much worse than today. People were unfree and starving, and lower-class women especially had no choice, no hope, nothing at all. Girls who went into domestic service had an absolutely horrible time: they had just one day – 12 hours – free in a fortnight, and if they didn't know anyone you can imagine what that meant. Twelve hours – worse than slavery! That was the situation in America before 1914, and until about 1920 in Europe. So today we are in a much better world, but it is a world threatened by our mad education of children. We have to act on this, and once we have achieved a very responsible type of education we can go back to the days when violence was rare. As things stand today, however, violence is becoming more and more the daily bread: people are hardly interested in anything else.

*But how can we get political action off the ground to achieve these aims? With what energies? How can people's agreement with such priorities actually be mobilized? Here we come up against a tradi-tional objection to liberalism: namely, that it is too weak to get the better of opposing forces, of opposing passions, interests and beliefs.*

To the traditional objection, I reply with the traditional liberal answer: that we have to oppose violence. Just consider that thirty years ago, there would not have been any party in favour of violence; everybody would have agreed that we want a world without violence. But today this self-evident assumption has almost been forgotten. The case with that boy's fan mail in Italy shows that violence is a real danger among children and young people, that they get into it as a kind of habit. A boy is admired because he kills his parents for money, because he can't wait, so to speak. It is a frightful situation, really. And we have created it: we have allowed this to happen. We saw it and we were so stupid that we did not protest. Now it is high time to do something about it – more than high time. We cannot go on like this.

*Religious people, the Churches, say that it is they, and not secular liberals or others, who have an answer to the problem.*

I am for cooperation with religious people. After all, they know themselves that they haven't been very effective in propagating their ideas. But of course there cannot be cooperation if they use violence, as fundamentalists do in Iraq, Iran and so on. I am talking of religious people who have the same idea of non-violence – Christians, for example, or Jews, if they are not themselves fundamentalists.

*Do you think, then, that liberalism needs to be complemented by religion?*

I would not put it like that. I think that liberalism can live without religion, but obviously it should cooperate with everybody. There is, of course, the great problem that nearly everybody has been deeply affected by Marxism. So now, with the breakdown of Marxism, the hope of socialism has disappeared. What remains is the idea, long taught in schools, that everyone is after money, after gold and oil and so on. For Marxism propagated the idea that everybody is an egoist, that everybody wants only to be rich and to have money and cars and arms and power. Only now there is no longer the Marxist hope for an ultimate good society – just a hopelessly egoistic interpretation of history which says that things have always been like this and ever more will be so.

*It is hard to argue that the danger of violence comes entirely from the Marxist conception of history and its crisis.*

There is a combination of factors. This type of cynical approach, which is characteristic of ex-Marxist teachers, combines with the displays of violence that we see in society. You can easily imagine the effect of all this on children.

I have argued in the case of Germany that historical interpretation has passed through three periods. First there was the nationalist idea, from Hegel to Hitler, that Germany is superior to all other countries and ought to have top place in the world. Then came the Marxist interpretation of history. And now there is the cynical interpretation. And just as, in the period from Hegel to Hitler, it was taught in schools that Germany must be on top, so today it is taught that power and money have always ruled the world and always will. This is absolute nonsense. The opposite is true. You have only to look at the history of the United States, where 800,000 people died for the freedom of Black people.

*One of the most serious causes now of violence and war seems to be nationalism. How do you view the growing aspiration to form independent states, including in Europe? As a danger of war and regression? Or more as a right of nations with a homogeneous language, ethnicity or religion to have a state of their own?*

The key issue is that in a world as densely populated as it is now, all the problems raised by nationalism have to be considered dangerous. Dangerous to all, dangerous to the rule of law. First, there is a point which, to my knowledge, has not been sufficiently considered in the European debate but which is central to the nationality problem: namely, the fact that national minorities must be protected. The whole idea of the nation-state is impossible if you do not first accept this principle. After all, Europe is the result of accidental immigration from Asia. Europe is a peninsula of Asia to which people were driven, and when they reached the Atlantic they were split up. Then the various pieces were mixed together again, so that today there is no country, except Germany, without its minorities. That is why the protection of minorities is so important; that is the angle from which it should be tackled. Not all minorities can have a state of their own, but they should be protected in ways that satisfy their demands with regard to education, language and religion.

# 5

# ONCE MORE AGAINST HISTORICISM

## The future is open

*You have always attached crucial importance to conceptions of history. Your attack on historicism, in particular, has always been sharp and hard-hitting. This is one reason why, at certain times and in certain cultural milieux – Italy, for example, after the war and again in the 1960s and 1970s – your work was generally not well received. I myself admit that although I was attracted by many of your ideas when I read them as a young man, I found your anti-historicism thoroughly off-putting. Your critique of totalitarian systems seemed very convincing, but I refused to accept the enormous charges you levelled against historicism, and especially Marxism. After all, it did seem to me possible to be at once historicist and democratic.*

Historicism is altogether wrong. The historicist sees history as a kind of river coming down from its source, and he believes he can see where it is going next. He thinks he is very clever in being able to anticipate the future. But that is morally a quite wrong attitude. You can study history as much as you want, but the river or anything like that will always be just a metaphor. It has no reality in it. You study what has been in the past, but now that is over and you cannot anticipate anything in order to help it along or for you yourself to swim along with it. All we can do is act in the present and try to make things better.

*Agreed, someone who says: 'I always knew it would end that way' is a very unpleasant type of person. But when I read your autobiography, and again at the beginning of this interview when you spoke of meeting the Eisler brothers as a 17-year-old, I wondered what effect it has had to see so many things vindicate the criticisms you made so long ago. You were still practically a boy when you first formulated your critique of Marxism. For decades you must have thought: 'I am right', before or after others came round to the same view. During the last few months, haven't you ever wanted to say: 'I always knew the river would pass this way'?*

I am glad things have worked out as they have, but I don't feel happy today that I have always known where the error lay. That is nothing. Whatever has been is gone. From this moment on, our duty is to look and think what is the best thing we can do, to make things better from now on. We can certainly learn from the past, but we can never project it to anticipate the future.

This also has something to do with the terrible decline in art. I mean, whoever has seen the great works of the past – Michelangelo's, for instance – must admit that there has been a decline in art. Obviously Michelangelo was and will remain the greatest, and we cannot expect anything like that today. But what is the reason for the general decline in art? It is because all artists hear what historicists predict about the future and then, instead of trying to create good work, they concentrate on becoming leaders for the future. They are much too interested in themselves, rather than in the quality of their work, and they listen to bad prophets, bad philosophers, who themselves try to be ahead of their time. So everyone is trying to be ahead of their time, but in reality no one is in a position to anticipate the future. Look at Marx. He thought that all machines would always be steam-driven, and that they would go on getting bigger. Something like my electric shaver would have been impossible for him to imagine. But instead of becoming bigger all the time, machines seem to be getting smaller and smaller – and for our own personal use. Again, Marx saw history in terms of the means of production. But insofar as history is connected with material things, it is a question of things to consume, and these get better and better. The first railways, for example, were not built in the interests of production or the transport of things, but for the transport of people. There had been horse-driven coaches for passengers, the post and so on, and then suddenly you could have as many as ten coaches hanging on to one another and pulled by a steam engine. In fact, 'coach' is still the term used for them in this country. So, this made travelling much cheaper than before. It was a personal service for people going to see their relations, to visit other towns, or perhaps museums, and so on. Do you understand what that means? A personal service – that was the greatest revolution so far. But Marx did not see it as a revolution.

Then there came the Henry Ford revolution, which made motor cars available not only to millionaires but to workers. These are the great revolutions, and they cannot be foreseen by anybody. Certainly they were not seen by Marx at all. And nobody can anticipate what will be the next great invention in terms of personal services. One of these became a great horror, although it could have been a great blessing, and that was television. Incidentally, I don't have a television myself.

*So, you would conclude from this look at the technological revolutions that there is no basis for the historicist claim to know the course of the river?*

It is simply idiotic. It tries to foresee, whereas the real thing in history is always the revolution that is unforeseeable – the electronics revolution, for example.

*But it is very human to pose the problem of the meaning or direction of history, or, as we might also call it, the problem of the philosophy of history. If we can ask with some scientific basis questions about the dimensions of the universe, why can we not also ask about the meaning of history, about whether it is moving in a recognizable direction?*

I think this is an intellectual mistake. We don't need any meaning of history. We can admire history, because there is a lot to be admired in it, a lot of wonderful people. We can also learn from history what is to be feared, and among the things to be feared is what you call the meaning of history. Because it always misleads, and only misleads.

*In Russia in recent years, there has been a debate about what they call the 'point of entry', the point at which the 'mistake' or negative processes began. Now this appears to have been superseded by the facts, but the idea was to use it to find the 'point of exit', the way out of the mistake. I would like to know what you think about this, and why you perhaps place the 'point of entry' further back than anyone else.*

I have already said that in my view Marxism was a mistake from the very start, because the Marxist idea was to help mankind along by finding the enemy instead of by finding friends. You and I, for example, are concerned to cooperate in helping mankind to find good solutions to its main problems. Marx, on the other hand, wanted to find the enemy that had to be slain – and he invented capitalism as that enemy. One can see how, from Marx to Khrushchev, this was the great mistake. There was no 'point of entry': it was a mistake from the very start; hatred instead of responsibility. All those who had great ambitions and hated the world because they could not achieve them – these were the ones who made the great mistake. So, it is quite wrong to think that everything might have been all right if certain things had been done differently.

*I had no doubt that you thought the mistake lay in Marx from the very beginning. What I was not sure about, was the idea that it went back further still, to Plato and Aristotle.*

Yes, it goes back a long way before Marx. I have already said what I think of historicism. We could go into the origins of the teleological view of history, of totalitarianism and the myth of destiny. But we would only be going back over what I wrote in *The Open Society.*

*Let us turn then to a question of today – the question of democracy. Since the collapse of communism, we have a great degree of convergence. But although we may agree on certain basic principles of freedom, democracy is still a field full of problems, contradictions and difficulties. In fact you yourself quite often speak of the paradoxes of democracy. What are they?*

This is a very important point. If the term 'democracy' is taken in the literal meaning of the Greek word, 'rule of the people', then it leads us away from the essential problem. For the key point of democracy is the avoidance of dictatorship, or, in other words, the avoidance of unfreedom, the avoidance of a form of rule that is not the rule of law. That is the problem. And already in ancient times, the Greeks knew that democracy does not mean rule by the people, but rather avoidance of the danger of tyranny. That is why, for eighty years or so, they introduced the practice of ostracism. They were afraid of a popular tyrant or dictator, a populist – as we would say today – who would make himself very popular and be swept into power by a majority. And the function of ostracism was to ensure that anybody who became too popular was sent out of the country. He was not regarded as a criminal: he had not been convicted of doing anything bad. It was only a precaution against having someone too popular in the country. If you read Pericles'

43

famous funeral speech in Thucydides, you see that that was really the issue at stake.

Now, as Churchill once said, democracy is the worst form of government with the exception of all other forms, which are still worse. Democracy is nothing particularly good; anything good in it must come from somewhere other than democracy itself. Democracy is a means of avoiding tyranny – that's all. It is also true, of course, that in democracy everybody is equal before the law, nobody is a criminal who has not been proved a criminal, and so on. All these principles are part of the rule of law, so that democracy may be said to be a way of preserving the rule of law. But it is not a principle of democracy that the majority is always right; the majority can make the greatest mistakes; it can even vote to introduce a tyranny, as it has done rather often. In Austria, for example (unlike Germany where Hitler did not come to power through a majority), more than 90 per cent voted for him at the decisive moment.

*We can say, then, that democracy is a way of regulating political conflict so as to avoid tyranny and dictatorship. But in the political conflicts of the twentieth century, have we not always found ourselves with a Left and a Right? Is this not a permanent feature of modern political conflict?*

I have already answered that.

*You answered by saying that the time has come to go beyond ideological conflict. But you did not say what you think of the roles of the Right and the Left, now that the ideological confrontation between communism and anti-communism can be regarded as over, or nearly over.*

I think my answer to that is implicit in what I have said already. The original function of the Left was to be for the underdogs, and that was very good. But then this function became perverted. The Left, for ideological reasons, continued to be for so-called labour, for the workers, even when the workers were no longer the underdogs.

*To conclude, then, what role do you think the Left should have in the period ahead?*

You have to look around and ask yourselves where is the underdog. I assert that today children are the only big class of underdogs. In brief, adults now commit their crimes in front of the children.

44

That is the situation we have created. But everything nasty and criminal that is done in front of the children serves as an example to them. We forget that all animals learn by example, by seeing and copying what happens in their environment. Let us try to act while there is still time.

# INTERVIEW II (1993)

# INTRODUCTION
# TO CHAPTER 6

## Giancarlo Bosetti

'What is happening in Bosnia is proof of the failure, the cowardice, the blindness, of us in the West. It shows we do not want to learn what this century should have taught us: that war is prevented with war.' Speaking at his home in Kenley, in the hills south of London, Karl Popper takes up the question he has most at heart: the threat of a nuclear conflict coming from the Balkans. At 91 years of age, the Viennese philosopher makes a great effort to preserve his health and his capacity for work. Two years ago, when I last went to visit him, he was deep in study of the Cuban missile crisis and of Khrushchev's and Sakharov's memoirs. On the question of the Soviet scientist's 'grave offences' – Popper holds him mainly responsible for the mega-H-bombs around in the world – he has not changed his views. Despite the later merits that earned Sakharov a Nobel Peace Prize, Popper considers that had it not been for him the world would today be a decidedly safer place.

There is a sharp contrast between the forcefulness of his ideas, and the modesty, exquisite manners and quavering voice of a man who seems to be growing smaller and more defenceless. In his shrewd look one senses a lifetime of encountering disagreement more than recognition – a long training to meet objections. And this is appropriate enough in someone who argues that knowledge advances through trial and error, and that a thesis remains valid until falsified by another thesis.

This time, his gaze travels beyond the 1970s. From present-day Bosnia, he refers us to the twenty years between the wars, to the writings of Churchill, and to Kant's principles in 'Perpetual Peace'.[1] He had already explained, in a short text published by *L'Unità* a few months earlier, his proposals to stop the massacres in the former Yugoslavia. Europe, the United States and the United Nations should intervene not only with humanitarian aid but also with military force. 'To do nothing is inhuman and morally wrong.' Today the situation is even worse: nothing has been done, Clinton's wavering has been 'disastrous', and we are responsibile for letting happen things which undermine civil order on our planet. Popper fully shares the view expressed by a famous and ultra-wealthy student of his, the Hungarian-American financier George Soros, in an appeal published in August 1992 in *The Times*. If ethnic identity becomes a state doctrine and a criterion for citizenship, he argues, this will violate a human right and threaten the basis of our civilization. It is being used to justify the destruction of rival groups. And a chain reaction may spread out to engulf the whole planet.

# 6

# 'WE ARE IN DANGER OF A THIRD WORLD WAR'

*In April we published your text arguing for intervention in Bosnia. Have you not changed your mind since then?*

It was certainly no accident that I called then for intervention. And the problem is still the same: we must fight against war. The essence of the idea of 'war on war' can already be found in Kant, in his 'Perpetual Peace' essay. Perhaps we have forgotten the general feeling after the First World War that things should never again come to war, that the recent conflict had been a senseless sacrifice of human lives, a huge effort with results seemingly close to zero. Yet even during the years of fighting, the idea of a war fought against war had made its appearance. Of course, it lends itself to many paradoxes and is often used in questionable ways, but it is essentially a very serious idea.

*How is the 'war on war' principle to be applied?*

The Second World War was from the beginning conceived as precisely that: a war on war. The period stretching from the First to the Second World War showed the extent to which peace had actually depended on the responsibilities of governments. Neville Chamberlain clearly assumed the task of appeasing Nazi Germany, and saw it as his main responsibility to make concessions in the name of peace. That is exactly how he saw his task. And so he helped Hitler for a long time, when he was already far advanced in strengthening Nazi rule.

*Do you mean it can be dangerous completely to reject war?*

I am saying that during those twenty years, war was outlawed in many declarations by European and American governments.

Whatever happened, there were to be no more wars: such was the general attitude before 1939. The League of Nations was a very serious organization which did valuable things in various fields. For example, it issued passports and documents for stateless citizens – a fact of the greatest importance. I mean, after the First World War a situation developed in which strongly humanitarian tendencies asserted themselves, as well as policies whose essential goal was respect for human values. If that was not typical of the First World War, at least it was the result of its end. This climate was still widespread when the Second World War broke out, being accepted and shared in large parts of the world. And later it led to the founding of Churchill's United Nations.

*What conclusion would you draw from this?*

In the world today, there is no politician in power who had reached full maturity and awareness by the time of the Second World War. That is one unfortunate result of the passing of time: whereas twenty years passed between the end of the First and the beginning of the Second World War, the period from 1945 to the war in Bosnia was very much longer.

*Nearly fifty years.*

That is too long for people really to grasp things which appear to them just as history, as the Napoleonic wars would have appeared to me at the outbreak of the First World War. Just ancient history...

*Clearly we have no Churchill or other politician capable of intellectually mastering, with the help of his own experience, the period stretching from the outbreak of the last war up to the present day. But why did you say just now 'Churchill's United Nations'? Why think of Churchill today?*

Churchill's idea was that, in order to have no more wars, there must be an international organization like the League of Nations or the UN which actually fights against war. Churchill's principle was subsequently disregarded because of the role of the Soviet Union. In fact, the United Nations had to depart from it by accepting that intervention was possible only if both the West and Russia were prepared to support it. And as Churchill realized, that was a defeat for his political line.

*Now, however, there is no longer either a Soviet Union or a Cold War.*

After 1989 I was aware of the risks we would be running, but I also had in mind better prospects for the world than the ones we have today. I wanted to protest against Sakharov's bomb. I wanted to criticize the terrible responsibilities which the Soviet nuclear physicist had assumed with the decision to complete testing of the 'big' hydrogen bomb. My own views, which you published in Italy, pointed to the dangers we had to face because hydrogen bombs developed by Sakharov were around in the world. But I also saw a way out.

*What was the way out?*

I thought that after 1989 we in the West should have said to Russia: 'Look, the West wants peace and we have succeeded in establishing it without instruments of terror, without anything like the systems that were there before the Iron Curtain. Come and join us in this peace.' The European situation was, in fact, so peaceful that nobody imagined we could see a return to regimes of terror. The same could be said across the Atlantic, of the whole of North America, as well as Japan. There was not peace in Africa, but there was almost everywhere else in the world.

*Obviously that prospect has faded.*

First, there was the very dangerous intervention in Iraq, where the issue at stake – the real issue at stake – was nuclear weapons. And now the world looks completely different. Europe is less peaceful than when it was held together under the pressure of the old organization of power. And since the collapse of communism, terrorism has started to spread in Yugoslavia.

*Why has this happened?*

Communism has been replaced by this ridiculous nationalism. I say ridiculous, because it sets against each other peoples who are virtually all Slav. The Serbs are Slavs, the Croats are Slavs. And the Bosnians are also Slavs, converted to Islam. The terrible thing is that we in the West have caved in by allowing things to develop as they have done in the last two years – with massacres, murders, heinous acts. We have given up the key elements of a Western

53

policy and abandoned our own principles, starting with the principle of peace itself. We should not have done that; we should not have surrendered. It was a terrible mistake that exposes us to a huge danger, because the weapons and means of destruction have increased, and because Sakharov's hydrogen bombs (at least 3,000 times Hiroshima, remember) are circulating in the world. But how is it possible that we – the groups in charge of our countries, the governments and oppositions – remain content with this state of affairs?

*How do you think this surrender came about?*

The only explanation I find is that what we do not manage to see in the real world, by means of television, appears not to exist for us. The massacres have been out of sight for us during these years, and so it is as if they had not taken place. In the same way, we have never seen a nuclear explosion, although it really is the kind of experience which cannot be had more than once.

*In the last few days a compromise has seemed near over Bosnia.*

After what has happened, there is no compromise which can lead to peace. That is absolutely impossible. We should have disarmed them. A nuclear threat to us all may come out of the Balkans.

*What can be done?*

We are in the relatively fortunate position of having a weapon – aircraft – which we can use in such a way that the number of casualties is kept to a minimum. Western countries have a huge superiority in the air. What I propose is the withdrawal of all ground troops. It is a mistake to fight for difficult terrain in a foreign country (as the Americans learnt in Vietnam). You can do that in the desert but not in the Balkans. Anyway aid, medicines – even doctors, if necessary – can be parachuted in. People can be carried to safety by helicopter. And a lot more can be done from the air, such as hitting armoured cars and any kind of heavy weapon. There are many signs that that type of action would have brought about – and might still bring about – a withdrawal of the armies. They will go on massacring each other as long as we allow them to do it. They will stop only if we seriously discourage them. And so far we have never done that.

*Do you think military intervention is still necessary, what with the attempts to reach a political agreement about the map of Bosnia?*

'Peace, peace', they say. But we should have learnt by now that peace on earth (at least until it has been established once and for all) needs to backed up with weapons – in the same way, and for the same reasons, that the police should be armed to keep the peace inside a country. You could never get peace inside a country by reaching a compromise with the criminals.

*The German philosopher Hans-Georg Gadamer, who is almost the same age as yourself…*

He is two years older than I am.

*In an interview with* L'Unità *he said in relation to Somalia that the UN should never have intervened with heavy weapons, that it should have limited itself to policing operations.*

To accept that principle would mean never to have peace. It is complete nihilism to propose laying down arms in a world where atom bombs are around. It is very simple: there is no way of achieving peace other than with weapons. Gadamer must have forgotten that principle of Immanuel Kant's – and maybe one reason is that Kant, unlike Gadamer or myself, never got beyond the age of 80. But look, I don't think that philosophers have any professional authority in saying their bit about this issue. For that matter, I cannot speak as a specialist either – nor do I wish to speak as a philosopher. I am just saying what I think, like anyone who has tried to live with an open mind over the course of the twentieth century.

(Published in *L'Unità*, 9 September 1993)

# INTRODUCTION
# TO CHAPTER 7

*Giancarlo Bosetti*

'The problem of television should be solved through control and self-control.' When I read over the telephone this extract from the Pope's speech on 'electronic nurses', and suggested that the arguments were similar to his own, Karl Popper replied as follows. 'That may be true. You already know my views about television. It has become an uncontrolled power, even from a political point of view. And this contradicts the principle that in a democracy all power should be controlled. But we also know that the best form of control is self-control – self-regulation involving both television actors and viewers. Of course, in a democratic system this is a question that is the prerogative of parliament.'

The Austrian philosopher, who is 91 years of age, returned on Saturday from a trip to Germany where political-parliamentary plans are under way for a 'Popperian' regulation of television – to protect children from the invasion of images of violence. But he denies having taken on any political initiative. 'The developments in Germany are interesting, but I remain very sceptical that people will see the "anti-civilizing" process unleashed by television.' There does seem to be growing interest, however, in Popper's ideas about television. Yesterday morning, not long after the press agencies had featured Pope Wojtyla's speech, the courteous but unyielding Mrs Melitta Mew had to fend off the television and newspaper reporters on the telephone. 'I don't want to argue either for or against what the Pope said', Popper explains to me. 'I can't do that until I have examined the text.'

The last time I was at his home in Kenley, towards the end of August 1992, he had begun like this. 'There are two things I have at heart: one is Bosnia, and the risk that international relations will degenerate into nuclear catastrophe; the other is television and its consequences, which are hastening the moral corruption of mankind.' Then he spent an hour on the first argument and an hour on the second. The interview that *L'Unità* published at the time concerned only the first part of our conversation. And I would not have published the second part – which appears below – if certain things had not happened in the meantime, up to yesterday's speech by John Paul II. For Popper's theses on television have found an audience in various parts of the world: his first interview on the theme, which he gave to me for *L'Unità* and the Marsilio publishing house in late 1991, has been translated into French and just recently published in France; and a few weeks ago, a conversation he had on the same question with Helmut Schmidt, the former German Chancellor, was broadcast on German television. Finally, the decisive reason why we are now publishing his fresh indictment of television is that he himself, the protagonist in this peculiar fin-de-siècle battle, replies there to his opponents and tries to keep the discussion alive.

When I met Popper, he began by reading out a quotation he had jotted down in a notebook. 'Remind your readers what I wrote on page 225 Vol. II of *The Open Society*: the rational approach means being prepared to admit that I may be wrong and you may be right, but that by a common effort we can draw closer to the truth.'

# 7

# 'TELEVISION CORRUPTS MANKIND. IT IS LIKE WAR'

*What do you have in mind when you speak of 'moral corruption'?*

Quite simply and straightforwardly, I have in mind the growth of crime and the loss of the normal feelings of living in a well-ordered world. In Europe, until not so long ago, we lived in a society where crime was a sensational exception.

*Are you not mythologizing the past?*

I accept, of course, that this orderly world was also small, squalid and, if you like, 'bourgeois'. But it was a world where you could assume – as I assume of you now, for example – that the person in front of you did not have a gun in his pocket. That is the world which is no more.

*But you, Professor Popper, have always been a philosopher of optimism. You have always made us think that, as Leibniz put it, ours is the best of all possible worlds. Do you no longer think this?*

It is true that I am an optimist, but not quite in the way you suggest. I have never argued that ours is the best of all possible worlds; I said that ours is the best of the worlds which have so far existed, despite the terrible wars we have been through. Everyone knows, of course, that the experience of war-caused violence has had very grave effects. In our own times, the Western world has made a huge and successful effort to improve things. But now there is an evident deterioration, and for anyone with eyes to see it is clear that it is due to the violence we constantly have before our sight and our mind.

*It is hard to believe that such a massive degradation could be due entirely to television. Does that not seem exaggerated?*

The fact is that there is no other cause. Wars introduce violence into society, but the last great war was fifty years ago.

*Let me tell you now of the objections I have heard expressed in the months since your interview appeared in* L'Unità.

But first I would like to tell you of a memory I have. In 1920 I was in charge of a nursery school, and something interesting happened there. The cook had a husband of whom it was said (I'm not sure but I think it was only hearsay) that he had been seriously wounded in the war, that he still had a bullet in his head and was prone to violence. And indeed, horrible things happened after I arrived there. Once he flew into a rage with his wife and spent a long time holding a kitchen knife like this at her. I stepped in and, with a certain audacity, managed to get it away from him.

*You?*

Yes. You shouldn't be astonished. I was very young and the only one capable of doing anything about it. I took hold of the man and led him out of the room. Even though I had no adult to hand the children over to, I quickly got them away from the place where they had seen one human being threaten another human being with a knife.

*Why are you telling me this story?*

Because it is an example of something 'very exceptional' in the life of those children. For each one of them, it probably remained the most serious event they had witnessed in their childhood and adolescence. You see, it is a practical more than a theoretical question. It is also highly likely that that man's violence stemmed from the war that had finished only two years before. And today, fifty years after the Second World War, children are being found dead, massacred or violated.

*I will put to you the first objection, then. The human race has a great capacity for adaptation to new and different circumstances. In fact, you have yourself always pointed to the way in which living beings are able to react to their environment.*

Yes, children adapt if they are constantly exposed to extreme situations, but their adaptation to violence is precisely the problem we are discussing. The most logical outcome of adaptation is a future in which they too will buy a gun. The second thing to consider is what is being presented in opposition to violence. Parents? But how many parents do that? Teachers? But teachers haven't a hope in the face of television. Television is always much more interesting, more electrifying, more involving, more capable of seducing innocent little ones, more capable too of playing on their better points, especially their interest in life. TV has an unbeatable formula: 'Action, more action' – that is the whole philosophy of TV producers. What can a teacher put up against that? Only the voice of reason. Television took quite a long time to develop and reached its full impact only in the past ten or fifteen years. Then it came rushing down like an avalanche. Teachers don't stand a chance of resisting it.

*Another objection is that television cannot be stopped. It would be absurd; it's like thinking of a world without electricity, without the telephone . . .*

Electricity, telephone, cars. But what does this objection amount to? Are not all these things regulated? Are there not very precise traffic regulations? Just think of the incredible danger of using cars without a highway code. Ah, I find that kind of objection too good to be true! Look, please explain that I want people who make TV programmes to have a kind of discipline and self-discipline like that which regulates traffic on the roads. We need a licence to drive, don't we? And if you drive dangerously they take it away from you, don't they? Well, let's do the same for television.

*There is also a liberal type of objection. You are the theorist of the 'open society', and you support the role of market economics. But when it comes to TV, you want to have rules of iron.*

But what does that objection mean? Does the market not have its rules? If an Italian publisher brings out a book of mine, does he not have to pay me royalties? Does that go against the 'open society'? In every walk of life there would be chaos if we did not introduce rules. Nor is that all. In order to function, the market needs not only rules but also a certain amount of trust, self-discipline and cooperation. So I return to my argument that television has an enormous power over human minds, a power that has never existed before. If we do not restrict its influence, it will go on leading us down a slope away from civilization, making teachers powerless to do anything about it. And at the end of the tunnel there is nothing but violence. I began to sound these alarms four or five years ago, but they have not had any effect. I know that no one wants to stop this terrible power.

*Maybe it is not quite like that, Sir Karl. At least more and more people are asking: what if Popper is right?*

(Published in *L'Unità*, 25 January 1994)

# TWO TALKS

# 8

# REFLECTIONS ON THE THEORY AND PRACTICE OF THE DEMOCRATIC STATE[1]

## LITERATURE, SCIENCE AND DEMOCRACY: A CONNECTION?

In Athens a free market in books began to exist around 530 BC; it was a place where handwritten books were put on sale in the form of papyrus scrolls. The first ones on offer were Homer's two great epic poems: the *Iliad* and the *Odyssey*.

According to Cicero's account some 500 years later, Pisistratus, the tyrant of Athens, is the man we should credit for the transcription of the Homeric poems. Pisistratus was a great reformer. One of the things he did was to institute dramatic performances: that is, he founded the institution we call the theatre. Possibly, indeed quite probably, he himself was Homer's first publisher: he shipped in the writing materials (Egyptian papyrus) and bought many educated slaves to whom Homer's text could be dictated. Pisistratus was a wealthy man who, on the occasion of public festivities, would offer the Athenians theatrical performances and many other cultural events. Later a number of other Athenians – entrepreneurs – also played the role of publisher. They were attracted by the fact that the demand for Homer's works in Athens was insatiable: everyone learnt to read by them, everyone read Homer. Within an incredibly short space of time, his work became at once the Bible and the reading primer of Athens. Very soon other books were also being published. We should always remember that there can be no publishing without a market for books. The fact that a manuscript (or today, a printed book) exists in a library is no substitute for market demand; and for a long time (two centuries or so) Athens was the only place in Europe with a book market. Corinth and Thebes were perhaps the first cities to follow its example.

Before, there had certainly been plenty of poets – and plenty of manuscripts. But literature (which requires the institution of publishing) was able to develop only in Athens; only there do we see a blossoming of writers, historians, political thinkers, philosophers, scientists and mathematicians. Not many of them were, like Thucydides, actually born in Athens. Yet Athens exerted an irresistible attraction on them.

Among the foreign authors who came and published their books in Athens were the scientist and philosopher Anaxagoras and his only slightly younger contemporary, Herodotus. Both came there as political refugees from Asia Minor. I don't think Herodotus had written his lengthy histories with the idea of having them published, but that was certainly what Anaxagoras had intended for his (rather briefer) natural history. Both of them, then, were still unsure about how publishing worked in practice; it had only recently been introduced, and no one at that time could have imagined the way in which it would grow in importance.

## FROM THE FIRST BOOK PUBLISHED IN EUROPE TO THE GUTENBERG REVOLUTION

The cultural miracle of fifth-century Athens was, in my view, largely due to its invention of the book market. And this invention also explains Athenian democracy.

Of course, it cannot be proved that the expulsion of the tyrant Hippias from Athens and the establishment of democracy were linked to the invention of the book market, but there are many things in favour of this hypothesis. The art of reading and writing (which quickly spread through the city); the great popularity of Homer and (no doubt as a result) of the great Athenian playwrights, painters and sculptors; the many new ideas that were discussed, and the intellectual development in general – these are all basic historical facts that were unquestionably influenced by the invention of the book market. And even if we were to allow that democracy established itself independently of all these things, the great success of the young Athenian democracy in the wars of liberation against the vast Persian Empire was certainly *not* unrelated to them. This success can be understood only in the light of the new self-consciousness that the Athenians had won for themselves through their extraordinary cultural and educational heritage, together with their independently acquired enthusiasm and taste for the beauty and clarity to be found in art and poetry.

It is anyway remarkable that Gutenberg's invention of printing in the fifteenth century, and the great expansion of the book market in its wake, gave rise to a similar cultural revolution: that which is known by the name of humanism. All the arts flourished as new life was breathed into the literature of Antiquity. A new natural science was born, and in England the Reformation led to two revolutions – the bloody one of 1648–49 and the peaceful one of 1688 – with which Parliament began its steady evolution towards democracy. In this case the link was more plainly visible.

## SUCCESSES AND CRIMES OF ATHENIAN DEMOCRACY

The Athenian miracle of the fifth century BC is made up of the extraordinary cultural, political and military developments that followed the introduction of the book market. These went hand in hand with the rapid growth of a quite matchless literature that would serve as a model for Europe in the future. Among the great events in question were two wars lasting roughly thirty years each. In the first, Athens was destroyed and yet emerged victorious. In the second it suffered crushing defeat. Here is a brief chronology of the major events:

507 Establishment of democracy in Athens.

493 Athens arms itself; a navy is created under Themistocles.

490 The Battle of Marathon.

480 Athens is evacuated and then destroyed by the Persians. All resistance is concentrated in the navy. The Battle of Salamis.

479 The Battles of Plataea and Mycale. The Ionian Greeks, facing danger in Asia Minor and on the islands, appeal to Athens for help; this leads to the maritime Delian League and so-called Athenian imperialism. Fortification and reconstruction of Athens.

462 Beginning of the 'Periclean Age': the Acropolis, the Parthenon temple. First Peloponnesian War.

431 Start of Second Peloponnesian War.

429 Plague at Athens. Death of Pericles. Intensification of the war.

413 Disaster in Sicily: annihilation of the Athenian fleet and army.

411 Collapse of Athenian democracy.

404 Sparta is victorious over Athens and instals an anti-democratic, terroristic puppet-government which, during its eight months' existence, kills more Athenian citizens than died in the last and bloodiest ten years of the war.

This is usually where histories of the Second Peloponnesian War leave off, and so it is easy to imagine that it was also when Athenian democracy came to an end. But that is a wrong impression. It was not the end. After eight months the Thirty Tyrants were defeated at Piraeus by a force of Athenian democrats, and peace was concluded between Sparta and the Athenian democracy.

But the Athenian democracy had committed dreadful mistakes – not only tactical or strategic errors, but also crimes against humanity, such as the destruction of Melos apparently without any direct provocation. All the island's menfolk were killed, and all its women and children sold into slavery. Beside that horrible crime, what is the unjust sentence passed at the trial of Socrates (a political trial where the prosecutor was the head of a party)? Thucydides, who was a general in the Athenian army, gives a detailed account of the events on Melos and describes them for what they were – a cynical and unforgivable decision, taken by a majority who knew just what they were doing and ought to be punished for their crime. There were many other cases of a similar kind.

In such cases there were no extenuating circumstances, but fortunately Thucydides also speaks of other decisions. For example, when Mytilene rebelled and broke its pact of alliance with Athens, it soon found itself defeated by Athens. The Athenians then sent a ship with a general who had orders to kill the whole male population. The next day, however, the Athenians were seized with remorse. Thucydides describes the convocation of a popular assembly at which Diodotus argued in favour of clemency. He won no more than a tiny majority, but a second ship was immediately despatched and the crew rowed non-stop, day and night, with such vigour that it arrived just in time to revoke the previous order. 'So narrowly did Mytilene escape', writes Thucydides.

## DEMOCRACY HAS NEVER BEEN PEOPLE'S RULE, NOR CAN OR SHOULD IT BE

You will have noticed, I think, that democracy poses major problems; it has done from the beginning, and it still does today. The most important and difficult problems are of a moral nature.

One problem that always causes confusion and assumes the aspect of a moral problem is, however, purely verbal: 'democracy' means 'people's rule', and so many people think that this latter term is important for the theory of the state forms which we in the West today call democracies.

The Greeks used various names for the various forms of state administration – evidently because they wanted to ask which of the possible forms of government was good or bad, better or worse. And so they arrived at five names for constitutions, according to the moral qualities of the rulers. This idea was much used by Plato, who presented it in the following schema:

1 and 2  Monarchy: rule by one good man, and its distorted form, tyranny – rule by one bad man.
3 and 4  Aristocracy: rule by a few good men, and its distorted form, oligarchy – rule by a few not so good.
5  Democracy: rule by the people, the many, the multitude.

In *this* case Plato identified only *one* form, which is bad because among the many there are always many bad people.

It is very important to try to find the problem situation lying behind this schema. We can see that Plato starts from a question that is in a sense naive: *Who* should be in command of the state? *Who* should exercise the ruling power?

This naive question can certainly be posed in a small state like the Athenian city-state, where all figures of importance knew one another well. And, no doubt unconsciously, it is still at the root of political discussion today. Marx and Lenin, Mussolini and Hitler, as well as most democratic politicians, have tirelessly pondered – often without realizing it – on this highly personal problem. And when they formulated general rules, it was usually in response to the question 'Who should rule?' Plato's reply was: 'The best should rule'; it was clearly a moral answer. Marx and Engels replied: 'The proletarians should rule' (and not, as now, the capitalists); they should really have command of the state; they should exercise dictatorial power! Here the moral element is a little hidden, but it is naturally the good proletarians who should rule, not the bad capitalists.

Of Hitler I do not need to speak. His reply is simply: 'I.' It is clear that, like his predecessors, he thought the question 'Who should rule?' to be fundamental.

Some fifty years ago I set out to bury this question once and for all. For it is a false problem which leads to sham and ultimately ridiculous solutions corresponding to moral imperatives. And from a moral point of view, it is highly immoral to regard political opponents as morally evil (and one's own party as good). That leads to hatred, which is always bad, and to an attitude which emphasizes power instead of contributing to its limitation.

It would seem that what we were originally interested in was to compare different forms of government, not allegedly good or bad persons, or classes, races or even religions!

I therefore propose that we replace the Platonic question 'Who should rule?' with a completely different one: 'Are there forms of government which are morally reprehensible?' And its opposite: 'Are there forms of government which allow us to free ourselves of an evil, or even just incompetent and damaging, government?'

I would argue that such questions are unconsciously at the root of what we call our democracies; and that they are very different from Plato's question about whether the people should rule. They underlay the Athenian democracy, as they do our modern Western democracies.

We who get ourselves called democrats think of a dictatorship or tyranny as something morally evil – not only hard to bear, but morally unbearable because not accountable. We feel we do something wrong just by putting up with it. But we are not compelled to put up with it. That was the situation of the conspirators in Germany on 20 July 1944. They tried to escape the terrible trap into which they had fallen when the Enabling Law was democratically adopted in March 1933. A dictatorship imposes a situation for which we are not responsible, but which we generally cannot change. It is a humanly unbearable situation. So we have a moral duty to do everything possible to prevent its coming about.

That is what we try to do with the so-called democratic state forms, and that is their only moral justification. Democracies, then, are not popular sovereignties but, above all, institutions equipped to defend themselves from dictatorship. They do not permit dictatorial rule, an accumulation of power, but seek to limit the power of the state. What is essential is that a democracy in this sense should keep open the possibility of getting rid of the government without bloodshed, if it should fail to respect its rights and duties, but also if we consider its policy to be bad or wrong.

The question at issue is not the 'who' one of rule but the 'how' one of government. The main point is that the government should not govern too much. Or better, it is a problem of 'how' the state is administered.

This attitude lay behind Athenian democracy, unexpressed yet demonstrably there. It is still our attitude today, or ought to be. Whichever group may identify itself with the people – soldiers, civil servants, workers and employees, journalists, radio and TV commentators, writers, terrorists or young people – we do not want them to be in power or to rule. We do not want to fear them or to be compelled to fear them. We want to and, if necessary, ought to defend ourselves against their exactions. Such is the aim of our Western forms of government which, through verbal ambiguity and force of habit, we call democracies. They are there to defend the freedom of the individual from all forms of rule, with just *one* exception: the rule of sovereignty, the rule of law.

## THE KEY POINT: IT MUST BE POSSIBLE TO DEPOSE THE GOVERNMENT WITHOUT BLOODSHED

My view, then, is that what counts in a form of government is that it should allow the government to be deposed without bloodshed – after which a new government takes over the reins of power. It seems relatively unimportant *how* this deposition takes place – whether through new elections or a national assembly – provided that it is decided by a majority of either voters or representatives, or perhaps of judges at the constitutional court. Nothing demonstrated the democratic character of the United States more clearly than the resignation, in effect the removal, of President Nixon.

The major thing regarding a change in government is this negative power, this threat of removal. The positive power to appoint a government or a premier is a relatively unimportant counterpart. Unfortunately that is not what most people think, and there is some danger in making too much of the new appointment; for the nomination of the government may be seen as the granting of a licence by the electors, a legitimation in the name of the people and through the 'popular will'. But what do we know, and what does the people know, of the error or even crime of which its chosen government will be guilty?

After a while we are able to judge a government or a policy, and perhaps we will give them our approval and therefore re-elect the government. Perhaps we can extend it our approval in advance; but then we know nothing, we cannot know anything, we do not know the government, and so we cannot assume that it will not abuse our trust.

According to Thucydides, Pericles expressed this idea in a very simple way: 'Even if only a few of us are capable of devising a policy or putting it into practice, all of us are capable of judging it.' This succinct formula is, in my view, fundamental. Please note that it discounts the notion of rule by the people, and even of popular initiative. Both are replaced with the very different idea of *judgement by the people*.

Pericles (or maybe Thucydides – they were probably of the same view) says here very briefly why the people is not able to govern, even when there are no other difficulties of any kind. Ideas – particularly new ideas – can only be the work of single individuals, even if they may be clarified and improved in collaboration with a few others. Many people are subsequently able to see whether the ideas were good or bad, especially if they have had direct experience of their consequences. And such assessments, such yes–no decisions, can be made by a broader electorate.

An expression such as 'popular initiative' is thus misleading and propagandistic. It is usually the initiative of a few, which is at best presented to the people for critical evaluation. In such cases, then, it is important to know whether the measures being proposed are outside the competence of the electorate that evaluates them.

Before leaving this question, I would like to warn of a danger that arises when the people, or children, are taught that they are living in a system of popular rule – which is not true, and cannot be true. For if they suddenly become aware of this, they are not only discontented; they feel cheated and let down, not knowing anything about the traditional verbal confusion. This may have a bad effect on how they see the world as well as in the sphere of politics: it may even lead to terrorism. I actually have known such cases.

## FREEDOM AND ITS LIMITS

As we have seen, we all in some degree share joint responsibility for the government, even if we are not directly part of it. But our shared responsibility requires freedom, many freedoms: freedom of speech, free access to information and freedom to impart it, freedom to *publish*, and many more. An 'excess' of statism leads to a lack of freedom. But there is also such a thing as an 'excess' of freedom. Unfortunately, freedom can be abused, as can the power of the state. One can abuse the freedom of speech and of the press, for example, by giving out false information or by instigating a revolt. In just the same way, the state power can abuse any limitation of freedom.

We need freedom to prevent the state from abusing its power, and we need the state to prevent the abuse of freedom. Clearly this is a problem which can never be solved by laws in the abstract; a constitutional court is necessary, and goodwill more than anything else.

We must accept that it is a problem which can never be definitively solved, or, to be more precise, which can be completely solved only in a dictatorship, with its principle of the all-powerful state that we should reject on moral grounds. We should be content with partial solutions and compromises; we must not allow our love of freedom to blind us to the problems of its abuse.

## THOMAS HOBBES, IMMANUEL KANT, WILHELM VON HUMBOLDT, JOHN STUART MILL

Thinkers both old and new identified these problems as they sought to ground the necessity of state power, and of its limits, upon universal principles.

Thomas Hobbes started from the premiss that without the state every man is potentially a mortal enemy of his kind ('*Homo homini lupus*'), and that we therefore need the strongest possible state to restrain crime and violence. Kant saw the problem rather differently. He too believed that the state and the limitation of freedom were necessary, but he wanted to reduce this to a minimum. He yearned for 'a constitution allowing the greatest possible human freedom in accordance with laws by which the freedom of each is made to be consistent with that of all others'.[2] He did not want a state stronger than what was absolutely necessary to guarantee every citizen as much freedom as possible, insofar as this was compatible with the least possible limitation of the freedom of others. He saw this limitation of freedom as an inevitable consequence of human society; it may be explained with the help of the following story. An American is accused of having struck someone on the nose. He defends himself by arguing that, as a free citizen, he has the liberty to move his fists in any direction he pleases. To which the judge replies: 'The freedom to move your fists has its limits, and these may sometimes change. But the noses of your fellow-citizens nearly always lie outside those limits.'

In a later work, 'On the Common Saying: "This May Be True in Theory, But It Does Not Apply in Practice"', we find a much more developed theory of the state and freedom. In the second part, which is directed against Hobbes, Kant sets out the 'pure principles of reason'. The first is

> man's freedom as a human being, as a principle for the constitution of a commonwealth [*eines gemeinen Wesens*], . . . [which] can be expressed in the following formula. No one can compel me to be happy in accordance with his conception of the welfare of others, for each may seek his happiness in whatever way he sees fit. . . . A government [that] might be established on the principle of benevolence towards the people [. . .] a paternal government (*imperium paternale*) [. . .] is the greatest conceivable *despotism*.[3]

Although this last remark (after Lenin and Stalin, after Mussolini and Hitler) strikes me as exaggerated, I am fully in agreement with Kant. For what he intends to say – against Hobbes – is that we do not want an all-powerful state that is kind-hearted enough to protect our life (which is in its hands) against the wolves who are our fellow-men; rather, the essential task of the state should be to respect and safeguard our rights.

This task would still be decisive even if – contrary to Hobbes's view – everyone behaved like angels towards each other. For even then, the weakest would have no rights against the strongest but would be beholden to them for their toleration. Only the rule of law can solve this problem and thus engender what Kant called 'the dignity of the individual'.

This is the strength of Kant's idea of the state and the reason why he rejected paternalism. His ideas were later developed by Wilhelm von Humboldt – which is important because many think that after Kant such ideas no longer met with any response in Germany, especially in Prussia and in the main political circles. Humboldt's book, *Ideas towards a Definition of the Limits of State Action*, was published in 1851, but it had been written much earlier.

It was through this work that Kant's ideas eventually reached England. John Stuart Mill's *On Liberty* (1859) took its inspiration from Humboldt and thus from Kant, and in particular from Kant's critique of paternalism. It was one of the books that most influenced the radical-liberal movement in England.

Kant, Humboldt and Mill all tried to establish the necessity of the state in such a way as to keep it within the narrowest possible limits. Their idea was: we need a state, but we want as little of it as possible – the opposite of a totalitarian state; we do not want to have a paternalist, authoritarian or bureaucratic state; in short, we want a mini-state.

## MINI-STATE OR PATERNALIST STATE?

We do need a state, a state based on the rule of law – both in the Kantian sense that our human rights are a reality, and in the other, also Kantian sense that the (legal) right which limits our freedom is instituted and sanctioned, as little as possible and as fairly as possible. And this state must be as unpaternalist as possible.

I believe, however, that any state contains one or even many paternalist aspects, and that these are actually of decisive importance.

The basic task of the state – the one we expect of it more than any other – is to recognize our right to life and liberty and, if necessary, to help us defend our life and liberty (with all their appurtenances) as our right. But that task is already intrinsically paternalist! Even what Kant calls 'benevolence' has here, right at the outset, a striking and undeniable importance. When we find ourselves having to defend our basic rights, we should not encounter hostility or indifference on the part of the state (the agencies of the state), but rather benevolence. In fact, the situation is paternalist both from above (for the state agencies that are supposed to be benevolent) and from below (for the citizen seeking help from someone stronger than himself).

It is true that the law, in its objectivity, stands above these almost personal relationships. But the legal principles that become actual in the state and its laws are man-made and therefore fallible, while the agencies of the state are composed of fallible human beings. Moreover, such people are sometimes evil, and we have to be content and even grateful – perhaps for long years of service – when they show us that 'benevolence' which Kant despised so much. All this shows that in these respects the presence of paternalism plays a complex role. Unfortunately that is how things are – I do not admit it willingly, but I think it is the truth. And disregard for this truth has led in recent debates to logical abstruseness and sometimes quite absurd situations. I am referring to the highly topical attack on the welfare state. In my view, this attack and the discussion it has rekindled are of great importance. But as often happens, the currently fashionable philosophy cannot, unfortunately, be taken too seriously. It tries to show that the theory of the welfare state, and all the grand ideas about its morality and humaneness, are really an immoral attack upon the most important human right – the right to self-determination, the right to be happy and unhappy in our own way, the right that Kant defended against paternalism.

The new radical attack on paternalism usually quotes the following passage from John Stuart Mill's *On Liberty*.

> [t]he sole end for which mankind are warranted, individually or collectively, in interfering with the liberty of action of any of their number, is self-protection. [. . .] The only purpose for which power can be rightfully exercised over any member of a civilized community, against his will, is to prevent harm to others. His own good, either physical or moral, is not a sufficient warrant. He cannot rightfully be compelled to do or forbear because it will be better for him to do so, because it will make him happier, because, in the opinion of others, to do so would be wise, or even right.[4]

This passage, not exactly felicitous in form, repeats the Kantian principle according to which everyone should have the freedom to be happy or unhappy in their own way. It thus condemns any paternalist intervention as illicit, unless this is motivated by a danger to the interests of a third party. No one – no relative, no friend, certainly no agency or institution (such as Parliament), no functionary and no employee – can claim the right to be the guardian of an adult and to deprive him of his freedom; unless a third party is placed in danger.

Very well. Who would say anything against this principle of Mill's? But can Mill's principle be seriously employed to defend freedom of action?

Let us take a much-debated example. Does the state have the right to order citizens driving a car to secure themselves with a seat-belt? Obviously not, according to Mill's principle – not even if experts consider it necessary for safety reasons, in the belief that it is dangerous to drive a car without wearing a seat-belt. But just a moment! If that is so, perhaps the state is actually *obliged* to stop the car passenger, as a *third party*, from becoming involved in this situation of danger. Is the state not perhaps *obliged* to stop the driver from setting off until the passenger has decided (in full liberty, of course) to fasten his seat-belt?

Another much-discussed example is the ban on smoking. Clearly, according to Mill's principle, no one should be banned, in his own interest, from smoking. But what about the interests of others? When government experts say that it is unhealthy – no, actually dangerous! – to inhale the smoke from someone else's cigarette, is the state not obliged to ban smoking whenever a third party is present?

The same considerations apply to various forms of insurance. For example, according to Mill's principle, it should not be made compulsory, under threat of prosecution, for someone exposed to danger to take out accident insurance; rather, it is a third party – such as an employer – who should be forbidden under threat of prosecution to hire someone who has not already freely taken out insurance. The issue of drugs has also been quite widely discussed in this connection. According to Mill's principle, it is clear that anyone of sound mind and of a certain age (whether this be 14, 20 or 21) has an absolute right freely to destroy himself by taking drugs, and that the state cannot deprive him of this right. But is the state not perhaps obliged to prevent others from creating such a terribly dangerous situation? And is it not obliged to ban the sale of drugs (as it often does do), on pain of the most severe penalties?

I am not suggesting that every issue under discussion should be treated according to the same method, but it does seem to be very widely applicable. (The case of the driver, so difficult at first sight, can be solved very easily. The state has a duty to require, under threat of prosecution, that anyone who makes a motor vehicle available to a third party – by selling it or hiring it out – should first demand that party to sign of his own free will a document in which he undertakes to pay a surcharge if he forgets to fasten his seat-belt before driving off.) I accept that it would do our state agencies a lot of good (not in their interests but in ours) if they were constantly reminded – through this prohibition method – that they have no right to force anyone to do anything 'in their own interests'. They could still give free rein to all, or nearly all, their paternalist instincts – more or less as it happens today – but they would do so in a better form and on the pretext of covering third parties.

Social security contributions would then be demanded not for our own insurance but for the protection of third parties, and everyone would be perfectly free to pay them without making any use of their own right to protection.

I accept Mill's principle in the following form. Everyone should be free to be happy or unhappy in their own way so long as this does not endanger a third party, but the state has a responsibility to ensure that uninformed citizens do not incur avoidable risks that they themselves are unable to evaluate. Thus modified, Mill's principle can make a rather modest contribution to the (extremely important) critique of the welfare state. Our legitimate interest in a mini-state has *nothing* to do with Mill's principle, but it does have a lot to do with the issue of the welfare state, because it leads to the idea of privatizing social insurance.

Finally, I would like to point out that there is another traditional function of the state which, although I would gladly define it as superfluous like so many others, unfortunately cannot be so described. It is still a most important function, and it cannot be entrusted to any private enterprise.

I am referring to national defence. Clearly this is in every sense a paternalist function, and its current importance rather deflates, from a philosophical point of view, all the anti-paternalist theories of the state. Such philosophies seem to nourish hopes that the problem of national defence can be eliminated simply by ignoring it. But it is a problem of the greatest importance and demands a very high price. It is the most serious threat to the idea of a mini-state. It reminds us of another function, certainly no less costly or important, which is closely bound up with national defence: that is, foreign policy. Both have consequences which make the mini-state appear a remote and utopian ideal, although that does not mean we should give it up. The mini-state continues to exist, if only as a regulative principle.

I would like to remind you of one more thing. A state that has a duty to defend the nation must watch over the military readiness of its citizens and therefore over their health. Up to a point it must even watch over the economy, because it needs to have considerable supplies in reserve, to maintain the traffic and signalling systems, and much else besides.

## THE RIGHTS OF MINORS

Unfortunately, however, *in principle* as well as *for moral reasons*, things do not work without paternalism. When the state recognizes the right of its citizens to be protected by the police against robbery, it must also recognize the right of minors to be protected in various ways, if necessary even against their parents. It thus becomes in principle paternalistic. The problem 'mini-state or paternalist state?' is replaced by a different one: 'no *more* paternalism than that which is morally necessary'. Instead of a superiority in principle of the mini-state over the moral claims of the paternalist state, we find ourselves back with the old opposition between state and freedom and with Kant's anti-dictatorial rule of not limiting freedom any more than is unavoidable.

## THE PROBLEM OF THE CIVIL BUREAUCRACY IS SOLVABLE. THE MILITARY BUREAUCRACY

An important point in any theory of the non-tyrannical (and thus 'democratic') state is the problem of bureaucracy, because our bureaucracies are 'anti-democratic' (in my sense of the term). They contain numerous 'petty dictators' who no longer have to give much account of their actions and omissions. Max Weber, a great thinker, was pessimistic about this problem and thought it could never be solved. I think that in theory it can easily be solved if *our* democratic principles are recognized – and if we honestly wish to solve it. The problem of the *military* bureaucracy, however, does seem to me insoluble.

The danger of an indefinite growth in military power that is not publicly accountable is one of the many reasons why I, being the optimist I am, place (and have to place) all my hope in world peace, however distant this may still be – hope, that is, in the 'perpetual peace' of Immanuel Kant. But now that I am on the subject, I should explain at once that *in the interests of peace* I am opposed to the so-called peace movement. We should learn from our own experience, and twice already the peace movement has helped to encourage an aggressor. Kaiser Wilhelm II expected that for pacifist reasons Britain would not decide to go to war over Belgium, even though it was its guarantor nation. And Hitler thought just the same about Poland, to which Britain had given guarantees.

# THE HOPE OF THE YOUTH

Our Western democracies – and in particular the United States, the oldest of the Western democracies – are an unprecedented success. This success is the fruit of much hard work and effort, much goodwill and, above all, many creative ideas in various fields. The result is that a greater number of happy people live a freer, pleasanter and longer life than was ever the case before.

I know, of course, that many things need to be made better. Most important, our 'democracies' are not clearly enough distinguished from a dictatorship of the majority. But never before in history have there been states where people have been able to live so freely, and to have such a good, or better, life.

I know that too few people share this opinion. I know that our world is not without its negative side: crime, cruelty, drugs. We make lots of mistakes, and even if many of us learn from our mistakes, some remain a prisoner to them. That is how the world is: it sets us tasks. We can live happy and content. But that should be said loud and clear! I hardly ever hear it said. Every day, instead, I hear grumbling and complaining about the terrible world we have to live in.

In my view, the spreading of such lies is the greatest crime of our age, because it threatens to rob young people of their right to hope and optimism. In some cases it leads to suicide, drug-taking or terrorism.

## OPTIMISM AND THE DANGER OF THE MEDIA

Fortunately, the truth is easy to verify: the truth that we in the West live in the best world that has ever existed. We cannot allow this truth to go unsaid. The media, which are the most guilty in this respect, need to be convinced that they are causing great harm. They must be persuaded to do their bit. The media must be persuaded to see and tell the truth, to realize the hidden danger that they themselves represent, to develop a self-critical attitude (as any healthy institution does), and to correct themselves. This is a new task for them. But they are doing great harm. And unless they cooperate, it will be almost impossible to remain an optimist.

# 9

# FREEDOM AND INTELLECTUAL RESPONSIBILITY[1]

The future is very open and depends on us, on all of us. It depends on what you and I and many other people do, today, tomorrow and the day after tomorrow. And what we do depends in turn on our ideas and wishes, on our hopes and fears. It depends on how we see the world, and on how we assess the open possibilities of the future.

This means we have a great responsibility, which becomes even greater when we realize the following truth: we know nothing, or rather, we know so little that we can safely define that little as 'nothing', because it is nothing in comparison with what we would need to know to make the right decisions. The first to grasp this idea was Socrates. He said that a statesman ought to be wise – so wise as to know that he knows nothing. Plato too said that a statesman, especially a king, ought to be wise; but he meant something completely different from Socrates. He meant that kings should be philosophers and that they should attend his school to learn Platonic dialectic (which is very learned and complex) – or, better still, that the wisest and most learned philosophers, such as himself, should become king and rule the world. This proposal, which Plato put into the mouth of Socrates, has given rise to misunderstandings. For philosophers were excited to hear that they ought to have become kings, and the huge difference between what Socrates and Plato demanded of a statesman vanished in the mists of philosophical dialectic. I would therefore like to explain the difference once again. For Plato, the phrase 'the statesman ought to be wise' is a claim for power on the part of the learned philosopher; hence the claim for power on the part of cultured people, intellectuals or the 'elite'. In stark contrast, the same formula means for Socrates that the statesman should know how little he actually knows and therefore be extremely modest in his pretensions. He will then realize his grave responsibility in matters of war and peace, and be well aware of the misfortunes he can bring about. He will know how little he knows. 'Know yourself!' was Socrates' advice; know yourself and admit to yourself how little you know![2]

That is Socrates' attitude, the Socratic wisdom. 'Know yourself!': recognize your own ignorance! Usually the Platonist is not a king but the all-knowing head of a party. And although his party may comprise no one other than himself, nearly all the heads of parties – especially of aggressive parties and of successful ones – are nevertheless Platonists; after all, it is the best individuals, the best-informed, the wisest of all, who Plato says should be our masters.

'Who should rule?' This is the fundamental problem of Plato's political philosophy. And his answer is: the best and also the wisest! At first sight this seems incontestable. But what if the best and wisest does not think he is the best and wisest, and so refuses to take command? Well, that is precisely what a Socratic would expect of the best and wisest. A Socratic would also think that a man who considered himself the best and wisest must be suffering from delusions of grandeur, and so could not be either good or wise.[3]

Evidently the question 'Who should rule?' is badly formulated. But right up to today, it has often been asked again in that form, and the basic solution has always been the same as Plato's. In ancient times the answer was: the emperor elected by the army, because only he can have the power to keep himself in power. Later it was: the lawful prince by the grace of God. Marx too asked: who should have power, *dictatorial* power – the workers or the capitalists? His answer: the good, class-conscious workers. And certainly not the riff-raff! They have to put up with being insulted. (In our part of the world they are no more.)

Most theorists of democracy have also answered the Platonic question: 'Who should rule?' Their theory has involved replacing the answer considered obvious from the Middle Ages on, 'the legitimate prince by the grace of God', with 'the people by the grace of God' – except that the words 'by the grace of God' are usually omitted, or else the formula essentially becomes: 'the people by the grace of the people'. That was already what they said in ancient Rome: *vox populi, vox Dei* – the voice of the people is the voice of God.

Always we find ourselves facing the Platonic question: 'Who should rule?' This still has great importance in political theory: in the theory of legitimacy, and especially in the theory of democracy.

It is said that a government has the right to rule when it is legitimate – that is, when it has been elected under the rules of the constitution by a majority of the people or of its representatives. But we should not forget that Hitler came to power legitimately, and that the Enabling Law which made him dictator was passed by a parliamentary majority. The principle of legitimacy is not sufficient. It is an answer to the Platonic question: 'Who should rule?' We must change the question itself.

We have seen that the principle of popular sovereignty is also an answer to the Platonic question. In fact, it is a dangerous principle. A dictatorship of the majority can be terrible for the minority.

Forty-four years ago I published a book: *The Open Society and Its Enemies*. I had written it as my contribution to the Second World War. In it I proposed replacing the Platonic question 'Who should rule?' with a radically different one: 'How can we draw up the constitution in such a way that we are able to get rid of the government without bloodshed?' This question places the stress not upon the mode of *electing* a government but upon the possibility of *removing* it.

The word 'democracy' – which etymologically means 'people's rule' – is unfortunately dangerous. Every member of the people knows that he does not rule, and so he feels that democracy is a fraud. This is where the danger lies. It is important that people learn from school that 'democracy', ever since Athenian times, has been the traditional name for a constitution to *prevent* a dictatorship, a *tyrannis*. Dictatorship or *tyrannis* is the worst thing, as we have seen once more in China. We cannot get rid of it without bloodshed, and usually not even *with* bloodshed. Today's dictators are still too strong – as we could observe in the anti-Hitler revolt of 20 July 1944.

But every dictatorship is immoral. Every dictatorship is morally wrong. This is the basic moral principle for democracy, understood as the form of state in which the government can be removed without bloodshed. Dictatorship is morally wrong because it condemns the citizens of the state – against their better judgement and against their moral convictions – to collaborate with evil if only through their silence. It strips man of moral responsibility, without which he is only a half, a hundredth of a man. It transforms any attempt to assume one's human responsibility into an attempted suicide.

We can show historically that Athenian democracy, at least with Pericles and Thucydides, was already not so much popular sovereignty as an attempt to avoid tyranny at all costs. The price was high, perhaps too high, and the democracy was abolished after less than a hundred years. The price was that often misunderstood process of ostracism whereby any citizen, if he became too popular, could and should be removed, precisely because of his popularity. In this way the most expert statesmen such as Aristides and Themistocles were sent into exile. It would be absurd to suggest that Aristides was banished because he stood in the way of Themistocles, or because his epithet 'the just' made his fellow-citizens jealous. That is not how things were. His epithet indicated that Aristides was popular, too popular, and the function of ostracism was precisely to forestall the rise of a populist dictator. That was the only reason for his exile, and for that of Themistocles too.

Pericles himself seems to have been aware that Athenian democracy was not people's rule and that this could not exist. In his famous speech that we can read in Thucydides, he said: 'Although only a few are capable of devising a policy, all are certainly capable of judging it.' But this means: we cannot all govern and be in charge, but we can all take part in judging the government, we can all have the role of jurors.

That, in my view, is precisely what election day should be: not a day that legitimates the new government, but a day on which we sit in judgement on the old government – the day when it has to account for what it has done.

I would now like to show briefly that this difference between democracy as popular rule and democracy as popular judgement is by no means purely verbal but also has practical effects. This can be seen in the fact that the idea of popular rule leads to support for proportional representation. The argument here is that every current of opinion, every small party, should be represented so that popular representation is a mirror of the people and the idea of popular government becomes as far as possible a reality. I have even read the dreadful proposal to allow every citizen, simply by pressing an electronic button, to vote directly on every point debated by his or her representatives on a television screen. It is also said that, from the point of view of democracy as popular rule, citizens' initiatives should be seen in a very positive light.

If we think of democracy as popular judgement, however, the situation looks rather different. In my opinion, the proliferation of parties is a very bad thing, and so too is proportional representation at elections. The fragmentation of parties leads to coalition governments in which no one takes responsibility before the people's court, because nothing is ever more than a compromise. It also becomes uncertain whether a government can be removed, because all a government has to do to stay in power is find another little coalition partner. If there are few parties, governments are usually majority governments and their responsibility is clear for all to see. I do not think it is of any value that the views of the population should be proportionally reflected in the representation of the people, and still less in the government. That would lead to a loss of governmental accountability, because a reflection cannot be accountable to its original.

But perhaps the strongest objection to the theory of popular sovereignty is that it promotes an irrational ideology, a superstition. For it is an authoritarian and relativist superstition that the people (or a majority of the people) cannot be wrong or act unjustly. This ideology is immoral and should be repudiated. We know from Thucydides that Athenian democracy (which I admire in many respects) also took some criminal decisions. It attacked the island and city-state of Melos (not without previous warning, it is true), killed all the men and put all the women and children up for sale in the great slave market. That is what the Athenian democracy was capable of.

And the freely elected German Parliament of the Weimar Republic was capable of making Hitler dictator, through the constitutional means of an Enabling Act. And although Hitler never won a free election in Germany, he obtained a huge electoral victory in Austria after the forced annexation.

We are all prone to error, and so too is the people or any other group of human beings. If I support the idea that a people should be able to remove its government, it is only because I do not know of a better way to avoid tyranny. Even the version of democracy as a popular tribunal – the one I advocate – is by no means without its faults. Winston Churchill's ironic jest is very fitting here: 'Democracy is the worst form of government, except of course all the others forms of government.'

To sum up, then, there is not just a verbal difference between the idea of democracy as popular sovereignty and the idea of it as a people's tribunal, or an instrument to avoid a government that cannot be removed (that is, a tyranny). The difference also has major practical implications: it is important even for Switzerland. I understand that in the educational system elementary schools and

Gymnasia uphold the harmful and ideological theory of popular sovereignty, instead of the more modest and realistic theory of the need to avoid dictatorship – and I consider that to be intolerable and morally indefensible.

I would now like to return to my point of departure. The future is quite open; we can influence it. We are thus saddled with a heavy responsibility, and we know next to nothing. What can we do that is positive? Can we do anything to prevent terrible events like those in the Far East? I am referring to the nationalism and racism and the victims of Pol Pot in Cambodia, to the victims of the Ayatollah in Iran, to the victims of the Russians in Afghanistan, and to the recent victims in China. What can we do to prevent such unspeakable events? Can we do anything? Prevent anything?

My answer to this question is: yes. I think we can do a lot. When I say 'we', I mean intellectuals – people who are interested in ideas and therefore read and perhaps also write. Why do I think that we intellectuals can be of any help? Simply because we intellectuals have caused the most terrible harm. Mass extermination in the name of an idea, a doctrine, a theory – that is our work, our invention, the invention of intellectuals. If we stopped stirring people up against one another – often with the best intentions – that alone would do a great deal of good. No one can say that that is impossible for us.

The most important of the ten commandments says: Thou shalt not kill! It contains almost the whole of morality. For example, the way in which Schopenhauer formulated his ethics is only an extension of this key commandment. Schopenhauer's ethics is simple, direct and clear. It says: do not harm or injure anyone, but help everyone as much as you can.

But what happened when Moses first came down from Mount Sinai with the tablets of stone, even before he could utter the ten commandments? He found a heresy that deserved to be punished with death, the heresy of the Golden Calf. Then he forgot the commandment 'Thou shalt not kill!' and shouted:

'Who is on the Lord's side? Come to me!' [. . .] 'Thus says the Lord, the God of Israel. Put your sword on your side, each of you [. . .] and kill your brother, your friend, and your neighbour!' [. . .] and about three thousand of the people fell on that day.

(*Exodus* 32: 26–28)

That perhaps was how it all started. What is sure is that things kept on in that way – in the Holy Land and then here in the West, especially after Christianity became the state religion. It is a terrible history of religious persecution in the name of orthodoxy. Later – above all in the seventeenth and eighteenth centuries – other ideological themes and beliefs were invoked one after the other to justify persecution, cruelty and terror: the themes of nationality, race or class; political or religious heresy.

The idea of orthodoxy and heresy harbours the pettiest of vices – ones to which we intellectuals are particularly susceptible, the vices of arrogance, thinking we are always right, pedantry, intellectual vanity. These are petty vices, not as serious as cruelty. But even cruelty is not altogether unknown among us intellectuals. In this too we have done our share. We need only think of the Nazi doctors who, some years before Auschwitz, were already killing off old and sick people – or of the so-called 'final solution' to the Jewish question.

Each time it has been we intellectuals who, from cowardice, presumption or pride, have done the most terrible things. We who have a special responsibility to the uneducated are the betrayers of the mind, as the great French thinker Julien Benda put it. We invented and disseminated nationalism, as Benda has shown; we follow the most stupid fashions. We like to parade ourselves and speak an unintelligible language, so long as it makes a striking impression – a learned, artificial language we have taken over from our Hegelian teachers, and which binds all Hegelians together. Such is the corruption of language, of the German language, in which we vie with one another. It is this corruption which makes it impossible to have a rational dialogue with intellectuals, and prevents us from seeing that we often say stupid things and fish in troubled waters.

The harm we have done in the past is truly appalling. Have we perhaps become more responsible now that we are free to say and write everything?

I once wrote in connection with Plato's utopia that everyone who has set out to create heaven on earth has brought only hell. But many intellectuals were enthusiastic enough about Hitler's hell. The famous Swiss psychologist Carl Gustav Jung interpreted Hitler's hell as a gushing forth of the German soul. At the time he did not have to be too afraid, because he was living in Switzerland. But after Hitler's death, he forgot what he had written and began to speak of the deep-rooted wickedness in the German soul. Winston Churchill and Franklin Delano Roosevelt, with their Atlantic Pact, founded a new world whose bases had been laid by the young airmen during the Battle of Britain in 1940 and 1941, who had stared near-certain death in the face and sacrificed themselves for us. Since the victory over Hitler, instead of languishing in his hell, Western Europe has lived in the heaven of European peace, in the best and justest world that we know of historically. And if Stalin had joined forces with us, we would have today – thanks to the United Nations – not only peace in Europe and the North Atlantic but world-wide peace; the Marshall Plan would have become a world plan.

But when the new well-being had only just been established and everything was going well in the West, the great racket started up and intellectuals issued their curses on our wicked age, our society, our civilization, our beautiful world. Dreadful exaggerations began to appear about the destruction and evils we had supposedly caused in search of gain, to destroy as fast as possible what remained of a world that had once been so beautiful. It is true, of course, that all life is exposed to danger. We will, I assume, all die sooner or later. There has always been danger, for the environment too, ever since the beginnings of life.

For the first time since the formation of our solar system, natural science, technology and industry have made it possible for us to do something for the environment, and all scientists and technologists are working hard with this purpose in mind. But now they are accused of destroying nature. Meanwhile the wonderful Lake Zurich, and the vast Lake Michigan on whose banks lies the city of Chicago, have for some years now been made safe without any great fuss. Life in these lakes has been saved with the help of science, technology and industry, in the first venture of its kind since life appeared in the solar system.

The world is not easy to govern. Every animal species, every type of plant, every type of bacterium affects the environment of a species. Perhaps our influence is greater than it used to be, but a new virus, a new viral or bacterial epidemic, could still wipe us out within the space of a few years.

Nature cannot easily be kept under control. Nor is a democracy a simple matter. As I already mentioned, Churchill once said that democracy is the worst form of government, except for all the others. But I would like to add something that Churchill did not make clear. For the government itself, democracy is by far the most troublesome and difficult form, because governments are always in danger of being brought down. They have to give an account of themselves, to you and to me. This is very positive, but it makes their work difficult. We are the jury, the jurors, but there is a risk that we will be led astray by the irreligion that is now and again universally professed. Hegel's ever-dangerous *Zeitgeist*, the fashionable (and nearly always stupid) ideologies that turn true into false even when the truth is there before our eyes – all this leads us astray as jurors, as members of a jury.

Hitler had the opportunity, as I did, to learn from visionary professors everything they believed in the depth of their souls: that the world would be delivered from its ills by the German spirit, and then *Deutschland, Deutschland, über alles, über alles in der Welt*. And Adolf believed in that, together with many other impoverished young people, millions of brave youths who died in the two German wars for hegemony over Europe, dragging down with them into the grave still more numerous and valiant enemies. And those enemies fought with unparalleled courage for freedom and peace, as did young Germans for the greatness and supremacy of Germany, for the Kaiser, the supreme warlord, and for the Führer.

Today we can and should take stock of the truth. The German ideology was an illusion, as a great and courageous German historian, Fritz Fischer, has shown. To be even more blunt, it was a lie. The Western ideology – despite all the denigration and often mendacious abuse to which it is subjected – was the truth. The West fought for peace and achieved it not only in Europe, which from the beginning of human history had always been wasted by wars, but also nearly everywhere else where West Europeans had had an influence.

But irresponsible intellectuals have managed to see only evil in our Western world. They founded a new religion which teaches that our world is unjust and will inevitably decline. They began teaching it with Oswald Spengler's book *The Decline of the West*, because they wanted to be original and to say things that fly in the face of the evidence. And they succeeded in overturning not only the evidence but the objective truth.

But I do not want to go on blaming intellectuals. I would like to ask them to accept their responsibility for mankind and for the truth. Our freedom allows them to say everything, even to insult the free world and to paint it as an evil world. That is their perfect right, but it is not the truth. And it is immoral to spread lies, even if one has the right to do so. And it is not only immoral but irresponsible to endanger the great goals which Churchill and Roosevelt, the war heroes and the Marshall Plan accomplished – to discredit them and make good appear as evil.

I would like to remind you that today the Russians are also beginning to recognize our world and our peace, and to admit that a much broader peace is no longer utopian or beyond the bounds of possibility. We must summon up all our energies to ensure that these possibilities are not curtailed by lies about heaven and hell.

In the West, then, we live in heaven – the first heaven, of course, not yet the seventh. Our heaven can be greatly improved; so we should no longer insult or defame our world, which is by far the best there has ever been, particularly as far as Europe is concerned. The truth is that we are not satisfied with reforms already achieved – and nowhere is this more so than in the United States.

We are people of goodwill and full of forbearance. This was demonstrated by soldiers on both sides of the front. The basic conditions have thus been created for peace on earth. But it is a necessary condition that *the Russians should join forces with us*. If they do, it may be possible to achieve the dream of Churchill and Roosevelt – not only in Europe but throughout the world.

For the first time since the Second World War, it does seem that the Russians are prepared to cooperate! Sakharov, that great and courageous but lonely figure, says that we should not trust the dictator Gorbachev, who is still too powerful. Sakharov also says that the Soviet Union is close to breaking up. But we cannot wish for such a break-up, which would bring with it immense hardships in the Soviet Union and great dangers for the peace. It might perhaps lead to military dictatorship – to a dictatorship of the largest (though maybe not the best) army, navy and air force that the world has ever seen. And that would ruin the hopes for peace.

George Soros – who knows Russia well, though not as well as Sakharov does – has analysed all these dangers in a major article in the *New York Review of Books*. But he thinks that Russia really will seek to cooperate with the West. The Russians know better than we do where is heaven and where is hell.

To make such cooperation possible, we should first recognize in our own minds what we have achieved so far and what we have shown to be attainable in conditions of freedom. Only then can we ask ourselves how we have achieved it, and so offer the Russians our help if they are prepared to reduce their armed forces – all this *with every possible precaution*.

These possibilities are within our reach; they require us intellectuals to see the objective truth at last, and not, as before, to keep switching heaven and hell around.

We should know that we know nothing – or almost nothing – and that Gorbachev is in the same position as we are. To move even one step closer to peace, we must give up ideologies, and especially the ideology of unilateral disarmament which is such a threat to peace. We should cautiously feel the ground ahead of us, as cockroaches do, and try to reach the truth *in all modesty*. We should stop trying to recite the part of all-knowing prophets. But this means that *we ourselves must change*.

# NOTES

## INTRODUCTION

1 See the most recent edition of K. Popper, *Unended Quest*, London: Routledge, 1992.

2 See the recent one-volume edition, K. Popper, *The Open Society and Its Enemies*, London: Routledge, 1995. The first Italian edition was published by Armando only in 1974.

3 See Popper, *Unended Quest*, p. 35, where Marxism is defined as 'a historical prophecy, combined with an implicit appeal to the following moral law: Help to bring about the inevitable!'

4 Ibid., p. 36.

5 Due to be published in the Florentine journal *Iride*.

6 In Isaiah Berlin, *Four Essays on Liberty*, Oxford: Oxford University Press, 1969, pp. 118–172.

7 See the interview with Steven Lukes (note 5).

8 On this conception of the Left, see my *Il legno storto e altre cinque idee per ripensare la sinistra*, Venice: Marsilio, 1991.

9 Many investigations carried out in the United States, however, certainly provide food for thought. See the collective work, *Big World, Small Screen: The Role of Television in American Society*, Lincoln: University of Nebraska Press, 1992.

10 Cf. K. Popper and K. Lorenz, *Die Zukunft ist offen. Das Altenberger Gespräch*, Munich: Piper, 1985, especially the pages on how the human species effects change through risk-taking and trial-and-error approaches to the problems it encounters. The search for a better world is described by Popper as part of the 'adventure of living'. 'It is always our wish, our hope, our utopia, to discover an ideal world. That is somehow implanted in us through Darwinian selection' (p. 17).

11 I am referring to a research programme widely developed in Italy in recent years. See Giovanna Zincona, *Da sudditi a cittadini*, Bologna: Il Mulino, 1992.

12 See 'La superbomba del falco Sacharov', *L'Unità*, 5 December 1991.

13 I remember, among others, the response of Norberto Bobbio, who finds in Popper's words today 'an excess of blame', whereas there was perhaps 'excessive praise' in the speech he gave in 1981. Bobbio also regrets that

Popper's accusations do not mention the concept of 'deterrence', which characterized defence strategies during the period of the balance of nuclear terror. See his interview 'Difendo Sacharov. Non era un criminale', in *L'Unità*, 6 December 1991.

14 All these quotations are from K. Popper, 'The Importance of Critical Discussion. An Argument for Human Rights and Democracy', *Free Inquiry*, vol. 2, no. 1, Winter 1981–82, pp. 7–8.

15 A. Sakharov, *Memoirs*, London: Hutchinson, 1990.

16 Fedor Burlatsky insists on this point in his *Khrushchev and the First Russian Spring*, London: Weidenfeld & Nicolson, 1991, esp. pp. 257–262.

17 The exception in Italy was Norberto Bobbio's careful and detailed review of *The Open Society*, not long after its original publication in English. See 'Società chiusa e società aperta', *Il Ponte*, no. 12, December 1946, pp. 1039–1046.

## 1 PACIFISM, WAR, THE ENCOUNTER WITH COMMUNISM

1 K. Popper, *Unended Quest*, London: Routledge, 1992, p. 35.

## 3 THE YEAR 1962

1 N. Khrushchev, *Khrushchev Remembers*, London: André Deutsch, 1971, p. 513.

2 K. Popper, 'The Importance of Critical Discussion. An Argument for Human Rights and Democracy', *Free Inquiry*, vol. 2, no. 1, Winter 1981–82, p. 8.

3 A. Sakharov, *Memoirs*, London: Hutchinson, 1990, p. 218.

4 Khrushchev, *Khrushchev Remembers*, p. 493.

5 Ibid., p. 496.

6 Ibid.

7 R. Kennedy, *Thirteen Days: a Memory of the Cuban Missile Crisis*, New York: Norton, 1969.

8 M. Beschloss, *Kennedy versus Khrushchev. The Crisis Years 1960–1963*, London: Faber & Faber, 1991.

9 Sakharov, *Memoirs*, p. 221.

10 Ibid.

11 Ibid.

12 *Corriere della Sera*, 28 August 1991.

## 4 THE POLITICAL AGENDA TODAY

1 Popper is referring here to Pietro Maso, a 19-year-old from Verona, who killed his father and mother on 17 April 1991. Considerable attention was given to the case in the British press.

## INTRODUCTION TO CHAPTER 6

1 I. Kant, 'Perpetual Peace: a Philosophical Sketch', in *Political Writings*, Cambridge: Cambridge University Press, 1991.

## 8 REFLECTIONS ON THE THEORY AND PRACTICE OF THE DEMOCRATIC STATE

1 Previously unpublished text of a talk given in Munich on 9 June 1988 at the invitation of the Hofmann Bank. A version in Spanish was published by *La Nación* in September 1990.
2 I. Kant, *Critique of Pure Reason*, London: Macmillan, 1963, p. 312. See also 'Perpetual Peace: a Philosophical Sketch' (in *Political Writings*, Cambridge: Cambridge University Press, 1991) and other writings of Kant's.
3 I. Kant, 'On the Common Saying: "This May Be True in Theory, But It Does Not Apply in Practice"', in *Political Writings*, p. 74.
4 John Stuart Mill, *On Liberty and Other Essays*, Oxford: Oxford University Press, 1991, p. 14.

## 9 FREEDOM AND INTELLECTUAL RESPONSIBILITY

1 Previously unpublished text of a talk given in 1989 at the *Liberales Forum* at St Gallen University.
2 See Xenophon's *Memorials of Socrates*, IX.6.
3 Ibid.

# NAME INDEX